20,000
MILES

M^CNIDDER | &
GRACE

20,000 MILES

THE CAMBRIDGE UNIVERSITY
INDO-AFRICAN EXPEDITION 1960
CAMBRIDGE – COLOMBO – CAPE TOWN

Christopher Fenwick

Published by McNidder & Grace
Aswarby House
Aswarby
Sleaford NG34 8SE
United Kingdom
www.mcnidderandgrace.co.uk

First published in 2017
©Christopher Fenwick

A catalogue record for this work is available from the British Library.
ISBN: 9780857161796

Designed by Obsidian Design

Printed and bound in the EU by Pulsio Print

Dedication

To my father, Trevor Fenwick, for whom
I should have written much earlier.

To Robin and John, my firm and fond friends
and companions.

To all those who gave help and
hospitality along the road.

Author

Christopher Fenwick was born and brought up in Newcastle upon Tyne. After National Service in 40 Commando Royal Marines, seeing active service in the Cyprus Emergency and Suez landings, he attended Cambridge University, gaining a degree in Economics and History. Before launching his business career, he initiated the expedition described in this book. Afterwards he joined Fenwick of Newcastle and New Bond Street, London, his family's business of department stores. With his brothers and colleagues, he worked to rebuild both the original stores and form a national retail concern. Now retired, he has a chance to write down some of his experiences. He lives with his wife Paula in Pangbourne, Berkshire. He retains his season ticket for Newcastle United FC. This, and other matters, see him frequently back in the North.

Contents

Illustrations

Between pages 40 and 41

Naqsh-e Rustam

Two miles from Persepolis. A vast perpendicular rock face in which is contained the remains of at least four Persian kings including Darius I and Xerxes I. To the left is the rock relief of the Roman Emperor Valerian paying homage to the Sassanian King Shapur I after being defeated by him in 260 AD.

Islamic Architecture

Golestan Palace in Tehran, Iran, former residence of the Shah.

Humayun's Tomb, Delhi, India.

Badshahi Mosque, Lahore, India, one of the largest mosques in Islam.

The Sheikh Lotffollah Mosque, Isfahan, Iran.

The Shalimar Gardens, Lahore, India.

The music hall in the Ali Qapu Palace, Isfahan, Iran. The musicians would play, exit. Enter the Shah, and the music would play back.

Saint Sophia, Istanbul, Turkey.

The Taj Mahal, India.

Hagia Sofia, Istanbul.

Sultan Ahmed Mosque (Blue Mosque), Istanbul.

Between pages 80 and 81

Northwest Frontier

Mountain fort hewn out of the precipice.

A cold swim in the Band-e-Amir natural reservoir.

It is a hard life as a shepherd in Afghanistan.

Huge Buddha figure, at Bamyan, carved into the rock. Its face was removed in the 6th century; the whole was dynamited out of the rock by the Taliban since our visit.

Tea (or chai) at Band-e-Amir.

Waterfall at Band-e-Amir.

A bucolic Khyber Pass.

Chris, trained and well used to handling the British service Lee Enfield Mark IV rifle, was astonished at the equal quality of the facsimiles produced without powered tools at the factory in the Kohat tribal area in Pakistan. The metal work was fine. The bolt action inserting the round into the chamber was smooth as silk.

Inspecting the inside works.

Chris inspects a facsimile of the former British Lee Enfield service rifle.

Simple technology.

Shakira to Mr Meer's (on the left) factory.

One of his carpets.

Tiffin at Pahalgam where rises the Jhelum, grand tributary of the Indus.

John and Robin with Rahim in the Srinagar gardens.

Our houseboat.

Rahim, our houseboatman.

The Rajpath, New Delhi, with Government House at its end.

With Ali Tobraki in Tabriz.

Performing bear in Turkish town.

Sacred cow.

Elephant in Amber.

Rivers

Gentle Jhelum.

Kasimat, our Ganges boatman.

Flooded Jumna.

Disappearing temple.

Bathing in the Ganges at Benares.

Between pages 120 and 121

Caspian Robin: Robin shows his sense of humour as he proffers a sample of our consistent diet of Fray Bentos steak and kidney pie with his back to the Caspian beach. The sea is the world's largest body of inland water and occupies an area larger than that of Great Britain.

John making the first breakfast near Nancy, France. Note the use of the front seats of the car adapted for use as camping stools.

Central India was flooded with monsoon water as this road illustrates.

Caspian John: John ponders how to repair the car's hydraulic clutch to drive it from the Caspian's 90 feet below sea level over the 9,000 foot pass to Tehran and mechanical help.

A large truck stuck beneath the superstructure of a bridge in eastern Turkey forced us to make a detour along the old Soviet border and Mount Ararat to reach the Iranian border.

First trial for our 'Casino' tent: plenty of height, easy entrance.

A Tabriz (Iran) real family business as grandfather, son and grandson make ready to mend our rear suspension.

Caspian Chris: Christopher wrote the diary and letters home to be distributed by his father's secretary Linda Marshall.

John has his pipes bid farewell to eastern Turkey.

Dual-purpose toilet paper.

'I don't think so Chris'. Bartholomew's Maps and full discussion kept us on the correct road.

Ali Tobraki introduced us to a lot of people in Tabriz.

Wykehamists are everywhere! John meets some old school friends in Iran.

We had the RAF to thank for transport from Aden to Nairobi.

The Border Post between Tanganyika and Northern Rhodesia. Despite both countries being British Colonies, it proved the most awkward. The Officer demanded a deposit of £150 for transit through the country.

The grand Kariba Dam.

The mighty Zambesi harnessed.

The charming Kassim Lakhas who hosted us in Kampala. They were later expelled by Idi Amin and their glorious Kampala hotel forfeited to the state of Uganda.

Kissing the road as we reached Nakuru, Kenya and asphalt surface resumed.

On the equator.

The roadside menagerie made our African drive both lively and superb.

Victoria Falls: The force of the Zambesi made the water spout over the rocky brink before falling below.

Front cover photo: Tony Weaver

All other photographs by Robin Gaunt and John Maclay.

Maps: Bryan Kirkpatrick

Prologue

"Jump, Fenwick, jump! There's people behind you!"

I leapt and landed, as instructed by the Royal Marine sergeant, and landed on the required one foot square rock ledge. It was only a ten foot leap but – from a standing start, across a twenty foot drop, wearing full kit and carrying a rifle – I had found it daunting. With this leap I felt my physical ability, while not boundless, carried more conviction and confidence. It was the start of my youth. I had shattered a mental block and I would now approach minor challenges with less concern.

I had not wanted to join the Royal Marines for my National Service but had chosen the Navy. They found a weakness in my right eye. As a result they said I could be a sick berth attendant or a Royal Marine Commando. I chose the Marines. It proved a fine decision. They were excellent people. They trained me, taught me things, made me fit and made me do things I did not want to do. My time with them brought me friends and excitement. One way or the other I have maintained my connection with them throughout my life.

After training, I was sent to Cyprus to join 40 Commando where we and other formations were trying to defend a pretty island for the British Empire. Later, we were sent to invade Port Said in Egypt to recapture the Suez Canal after it suffered Egyptian nationalisation and was taken from the ownership of the governments of Britain and France. After a day's fighting, we captured Port Said at the canal's northern entrance, but the Americans forced a ceasefire upon us and we had to return to Malta, thence to Cyprus to resume our duties there. My service had strengthened my thirst for adventure.

It followed me when I went up to Pembroke College, Cambridge University to study economics and history. We were given lengthy vacations. After a while I grasped that these were the last periods of freedom of such length I should have before work and old age approached, and the secret of their utility was preparation.

This problem of making good use of the three-and-a-half month summer vacations had to be tackled. Some students got a job and worked, some studied and a few, like me, realised that the opportunity of such a long interval might never recur. In my first year's long vacation I worked for a month in my father's business, carried out a military parachute course through my membership of the Royal Marines Reserve, stayed with friends and holidayed with my parents. I studied a little. All this was pleasant and even exciting, but made no use of the rare gift of time. Time was lost; I had not been well prepared.

By the New Year, I was pestering my splendid uncle to ask his equally splendid American brother-in-law to find me a job in his Madison Avenue New York advertising agency for my second summer vacation. Bless them both, he did so. I joined the university's Canada Club, which chartered two propeller-driven, four-engine KLM Lockheed Super Constellation airliners that provided a £72 return trip to New York, leaving on the last day of term and returning at the end of the vacation. I had a job for two months as a marketing trainee in Batten Barton Durstine & Osborn (BBDO) on Madison Avenue.

This was heaven for me at that time. I adored advertising and Madison Avenue was its world centre. I leapt at the opportunity. My boss, Lou Hildebrand, afterwards a lifelong friend, sent me all over New York's five boroughs in a hired Chevrolet Impala that handled more like a boat than a motor car. It had giant fins on its rear wings and brakes that stopped the car within inches. That summer you could fry an egg on its bonnet when stopped at high wire traffic lights in Brooklyn. My job was to visit supermarkets and report on the success of promotions the agency had devised. This was right up my street.

I met a red haired girlfriend, who was kind and intelligent, at her uncle's mansion on Long Island. Her parents had a ranch in Wyoming to which I was also welcomed. At weekends we went horse racing, to Long Island or to Radcliffe College in Cambridge, Massachusetts, which she was attending; it all passed in a blur. At the end of the summer, I caught a Greyhound Lines, long distance bus to Pittsburgh to stay with my Aunt Joyce and Uncle Leon Hansen who had got me the job in New York. They were an outstanding couple. He was a real captain of industry, prominent in the Pittsburgh business community. He had owned and run a large advertising agency in the city that, amongst others, had the accounts of United Steel, H. J. Heinz and Alcoa, the aluminium company, all Pittsburgh based international businesses. He had combined his agency with BBDO, New York, and so had been able to secure my job with them. I bought a Chrysler Windsor for US$300 and, after a few days with them, drove to Toronto to pick up my friend, Clive Simeons, who had been working down a copper mine in Sudbury, Ontario. We planned to cross the United States together.

We spent a night in Toronto and then drove to

Cincinnati, Ohio to stay with friends, before driving on to Chicago to see John Fell Stevenson and his father, Adlai, who had fought Eisenhower in the presidential election of 1952 as the Democratic candidate. He had a sceptical view of youthful energy which drove all night then slept all day. I tried to bear this sensible advice in mind. Nonetheless, he and John Fell waved us off for an overnight drive to Wyoming and Alice's ranch. We arrived the next evening with a broken rear suspension. At half past seven we sat down (late) for dinner, played bridge, then saddled the horses and rode off into the pitch black night. The horses found their way back home about 4 am.

In the morning, we came across Alice in the middle of the front bench seat of a large car cuddled up close to a cowboy. Considering myself dumped we drove 100 miles to Jackson Hole to fix our suspension, then 1,000 miles to stay with Clive's warm hearted and hospitable Aunt Dot in San Francisco. All these places seemed "just round the corner" in those days. Nobody seemed very surprised when we arrived. There were no interstate highways at that time, just dead straight asphalt ribbons stretching over the hills ahead, interrupted now and then with neon lit signs visible from miles away with the invitation, "Eat here". Sometimes we did. The road went on forever, especially through the Sierra Nevada. It was a late dinner for Clive's Aunt Dot too, but she gave us a good time on the Californian coast.

The following Easter vacation, another friend, Anthony Kenny, and I drove to Greece. Yugoslavia had just been opened up by Tito's Communist government. He had built a motorway through much of the country far ahead of anything in Britain at the time. It stretched 500 miles from Ljubljana, through Zagreb and Belgrade to

Skopje-Niš, within a short distance of the Greek border. It was so good that we drove too fast too far and blew the gasket of the engine, a problem that seldom occurs today. We had to replace it with the charming guidance of Bill Fink, chancery guard of the British Embassy in Belgrade. He introduced us to a mechanic called Nick who preferred payment in Nescafé and tins of Nestlé sweetened condensed milk rather than Yugoslavian dinars. Greece boasted less speedy highways but in a day we covered the 312 miles between Thessaloniki and Athens. There can be no greater sense of arrival than driving into Athens and seeing the Acropolis and have it dominate the scenery throughout one's sojourn. Beyond Athens, we probed further into the Peloponnese to Corinth, finishing at Olympia with its temple and still green springtime grass ethereal in the evening light.

We took an Adriatic ferry to Italy and drove through France, returning within three weeks. With long distance motoring we learned that you had to keep going. We did.

Itinerary: Europe

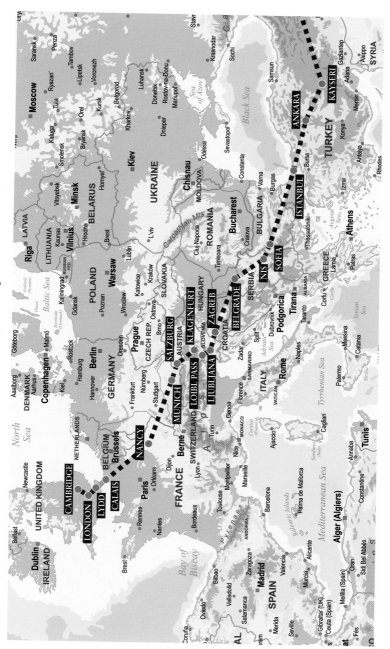

Itinerary: Turkey, Iran, Afghanistan and Pakistan

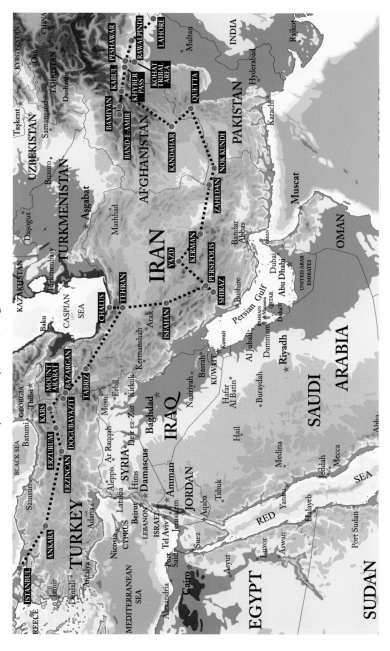

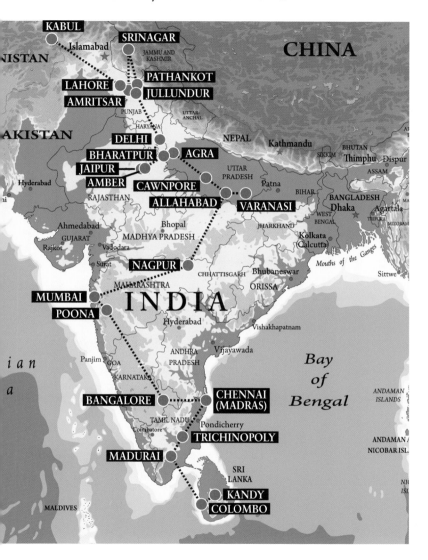

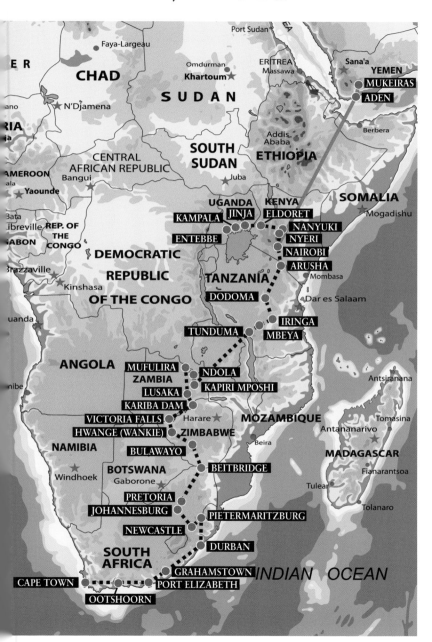

I

A Small Family Saloon

In my third and last year at Cambridge, I graduated with a degree in economics and history. Meanwhile, we had been planning our final summer vacation from early in the year, more open ended this time, as beyond us lay our future careers.

One Spring morning Robin Gaunt knocked on the door of my room in Cambridge. I think by this time he was impatient of endless options.

"Chris," he began in his definite way, "what do you plan for the summer?"

"I thought of driving to Madras," I replied.

"Splendid, I'm coming too." We were away. Robin's mind works as definitively as his speech, and however tentative my suggestion might have been, to Robin it was definite, there was no drawing back. But the trip was not just one idea but a succession of them. I went on to confess that Clive Turner had asked me to his wedding in Johannesburg. It would be convenient if we could also arrange a trip down through Africa to arrive in South Africa by the wedding day, 8 October. This readily agreed, I opened my diary, in which the publishers had thoughtfully included a map of the world for just such a moment. We planned our route from that.

Robin was of the right stuff. He was straightforward

in speech and thought. While his laugh would light up a room, anything slipshod would just as soon darken it. He was to prove a superb companion.

It was preparation a gogo. The more you can do before you cross the Channel, the more you can find out about the land you intend to cover and the greater will be the satisfaction at the trip's end. We did not have very much time, but we did all we could while trying to get our final exams passed at the same time.

The university doctor, Hawtrey May, made us give our expedition a name. We were behind a man in the queue who was planning to drive around the Mediterranean and who had an appointment with the doctor to seek medical advice for his trip.

"Who are you?" he shouted at Robin and me when we went in after him. "Are you going with Mr Hunter?"

"No," we responded "we're going to India and Africa."

"Those are different countries."

"Same diseases," I rejoined.

"Different countries – you'll have to come back another time. What are you called?" We gave him our names. "No, what's the name of your expedition?"

"We haven't got one," Robin replied.

"You must have a name. I've got fifteen expeditions listed here – one is called the Mali Expedition, another the Chitrali Expedition ... you must have a name."

"All right, the Indo–African Expedition," I invented.

"The Indo–African Expedition. Fine, there won't be another one of those. Come and see me on Thursday at two o'clock." It seemed a good start.

Now we had a name, we had to have some headed writing paper with which to write to prospective sponsors and helpers. Sponsorship was difficult, for the attitude of industrialists had changed over the previous few years. It used to be, "Where is the old British spirit of adventure?" Since then, the spirit of adventure had touched them for significant sums and they were not so keen to finance errant youth.

Although we were resolved, if need be, to go by ourselves, we felt it would be better to have a third member. He needed three qualifications: the time, the inclination and the money. We found several with the time and the money; the qualification most often lacking was the inclination. Finally, Robin's parents had a party to which came the parents of John Maclay. They heard about the trip and decided that John must come along too. John agreed and fitted well. He was laid back and laconic rather than a gung-ho adventurer, and could often see the bigger picture. We were all good keen drivers but John was an excellent one and had an instinctive understanding of the internal combustion engine. The shores of the Caspian Sea and the middle of the Baluchistan Desert were two places where we would have remained for a long time without his ingenuity. He was a Malayan campaigner and had been an officer in the Malayan jungle where he had fought the Communist insurgents with the Royal Highland Fusiliers. He was a hard man to stop.

It was 1960, and Anglo–American diplomacy was at its glorious best. It was a year of international travel freedom. Turkey, Iran, Pakistan, Afghanistan and Kashmir were all places to which a visit could be considered with equanimity. Visas were required but could be obtained. The same was true of Yugoslavia and Bulgaria. Aden, East Africa, the Rhodesias and South Africa were all under the British crown. The 3,000 foot Anatolian plateau stretching from Asia Minor to the Punjab upon which the countries of the Middle East sit is exciting and the treasures they hold brilliant but often mysterious. They constitute a "lost world" indeed. As for Africa, such a drive from Uganda or Kenya to Cape Town is perhaps still possible but less safe today. We also planned to include Eritrea and Ethiopia in our route but had to face crossing the Red Sea. Drives through such lands had already been achieved. To gain sponsorship, we had to think of a plus.

Many people had already made journeys in Land Rovers, so we thought that we would have a greater chance of support if we took a normal type of car – the so called "small family saloon". Moreover, with such a car, fuel costs would be lower and the capital investment less. But there was another reason, not financial at all but emotional. We wanted to do a drive that nobody had done before. We had heard of a Land Rover that had been driven from Colombo to London then down through Africa. We had heard of someone driving a Morris Minor to India and maybe back again. We knew of nobody, however, who had driven to India and Africa in a small family saloon. We wanted to be the first to do that, and maybe the last.

We chose an Austin A40. I bought it and exchanged the car I owned. It was the first of the hatchbacks. The novel hatchback body made it into a big cube to hold our food, baggage and equipment. The engine, gearbox and transmission scarcely let us down. The car's superstructure, apart from a bonnet catch, could not be faulted. It was the rear suspension and underside of the vehicle that time and again would let us down, use time and land us in a series of tight corners.

The converse of this was that through the mishaps we met so many local people who would help us. Without exception, they sympathised with our plight and did all they could to assist, often not charging us.

Murray and Charleton, the Newcastle-based Austin agent who sold us the car, strengthened the front shock absorbers and reinforced the rear by adding an extra main leaf spring. They fitted an additional petrol pump and a roof rack with a full tray. The theory was that the area between the tray and roof would make for more tolerable ventilation inside. We never took it off to prove this worked. The interior temperature at one stage reached 115 degrees Fahrenheit. We were proud of that. An oil temperature gauge looked good but was hopeless; it just made us worry. A large box of spares completed the equipment. We expected to load the weight of the car again on board.

For fuel we had the tank at five-and-half gallons, a jerry can at four-and-a-half and two four gallon sacs made of nylon and rubber given to us to trial by a manufacturer. They leaked in hot weather and stunk the car out. In theory, we could then carry 18 gallons, enough for 550 miles, but we were never short.

We also had the front seats converted so we could take them out for use as camping stools. The rear seats we removed completely and arranged things in order to sit satisfactorily on sleeping bags. Stronger front shock absorbers were fitted and extra leaves to the rear springs. An auxiliary petrol pump was installed. Apart from these adaptations our car was a standard showroom model. Still too standard perhaps, but the alterations were all effective.

For 1960, we had sound and practical camping equipment. We bought a quality so-called Casino tent. It had ample dimensions, not only for our three camp beds but also provided enough height for us to stand up. This means so much in a tent. After National Service, I had joined the Royal Marines Reserve. Their Tyne Division in Newcastle lent us camp beds, sleeping bags and two invaluable petrol cooking stoves. The day of the paraffin heated and methylated spirits ignited Primus stove had thankfully passed. The petrol stoves gave off considerably more heat.

We put much thought into our food supply. If one person eats a ton of food in a year then three will eat the same in four months. Our decision was to take enough meat for the trip and rely on local markets for fresh vegetables, rice and potatoes. So we bought three cases of delicious tinned Fray Bentos Steak and Kidney Pie. We began to believe that the only vegetable between Calais and Colombo was the runner bean. We should have learned how better to cook rice; we often produced either a dry ball or a soggy mass. Nescafé and Nestlé sweetened condensed milk made a unique white coffee. They also provided welcome gifts in poorer countries.

We had a smart blue medical box with basic plasters and bandages and complex cures for dysentery. We should have taken a Red Cross first aid course before departure, but happily we never missed this and looked to local help when we were indisposed. John was a good bagpipe player and he brought his bagpipes.

There was little doubt about our route's direction. That was painted on the car:

Cambridge – Colombo – Cape Town
Cambridge Indo–African Expedition

We bought Bartholomew's maps and noted where there might be options in direction and possible detours. We decided to include Ethiopia in our scheme, planning to cross from Colombo in Ceylon (now Sri Lanka) to Aden and thence across the Red Sea to Massawa, Eritrea and into Ethiopia, instead of crossing directly from Bombay (Mumbai) to Mombasa as we had originally thought. We felt that our new plan, tracing two subcontinents, would make more of a trip of it.

To begin, we planned to drive through Europe to Istanbul in four days and then take things more easily, stopping when we felt inclined and at what travel brochures call "places of interest". From Istanbul we would drive through Turkey and Iran to Quetta, Pakistan, from where we would loop northwards into Afghanistan by way of Kandahar, Kabul and the Khyber Pass. The Khyber Pass would bring us into Peshawar and Pakistan again, and from there we would drive through to India and south to Ceylon. Crossing by sea to Aden by finding a liner in Colombo and finding a cargo ship in Aden, we thus hoped to be in Johannesburg in time for the wedding on 8 October. What a milestone and target that proved for us! Clive Turner's invitation did much for our determination.

Robin pointed out the decision to be taken in Tehran. Eastern Iran is dominated by the great salt deserts of Dasht-e Kavir and Dasht-e Lut. Motor travellers have to decide whether to go north or south of them. So the decision was whether to turn due east and travel north of them through the holy city of Mashhad and continue to enter Afghanistan towards Herat. The alternative was to continue in the south-eastern direction initiated by the Tabriz–Tehran road. This would take us to the brilliant cities of Isfahan and Shiraz and past Persepolis, all the while parallel with the Zagros Mountains. At Persepolis we would turn due east and trace the southern route, south of the great deserts, passing Kerman (city of the carpets) and the lesser towns of Bam and Zahedan, going on to the Baluchistan Desert and Quetta in Pakistan, passing the frontier post of Nok Kundi.

These cities in Iran are in truth oases, so very natural points at which to build cities. In this way, Iran is much like Texas and the people have the same sense of exaggeration as the Texans: they are charming and claim that any project in Iran is the biggest and the best in the world. In terms of sightseeing, the southern route clearly offered more and we took it. Beyond Nok Kundi, Quetta, the first important town in Pakistan, was a day's drive at which point we would turn north to Kandahar, allowing us to tour a much greater area of Afghanistan than we would have been offered by the northern route. We chose not to be armed, reasoning that if we were we might find ourselves overwhelmed by numbers and encourage rather than discourage aggression. Furthermore, unarmed we might have less trouble at border controls.

Despite our attempts to have everything prepared well beforehand we still had a hectic eve-of-departure rush. Robin had obtained all the visas in good time. Mr Myers, manager of the West End overseas branch of the Midland Bank, had arranged currency and letters of credit. We had told Thomas Cook two months before that we wanted a ship from Colombo to Aden. They had done little about it. We had to leave the country hoping that we would be able to fix something in Colombo, where we discovered that there were in fact three P&O liners leaving Colombo for Aden within four days. We had been told there would be none at all. "Go direct to the carriers" was the rule, and we had not.

We were constantly collecting information about the places we were to visit, and we set off with a wad of travel brochures and many notes we had taken. I was appointed letter writer, and on the last day I bought a typewriter so

I could write while on the move.

In the evening we gave our parents a farewell dinner and went to bed as soon as we could. We rose at quarter past four on 17 June 1960. Robin went to fetch the car. He walked out from our flat in Charles Street, Mayfair dressed in grey trousers and a white polo neck sweater with two cameras slung round his neck. He noticed two surly looking characters were following him. He quickened his pace, as did they, then he began to run. They caught him up and stopped him. They produced cards and said they were policemen and suspected him of stealing the cameras. They allowed him to return with them to the flat where he was much relieved to find John who could identify him. All seemed set for an eventful trip!

We had driven down from Cambridge during the week so the starting point of our expedition had been fulfilled. We departed on a Friday, reaching Istanbul very late the following Monday night. This long weekend was all we had to enjoy of a lush, green and warm European summer that year. We had several agreeable memories of it.

II

Gone

We drove down to Lydd in Kent to catch the convenient, but eventually unprofitable, Silver City Airways car ferry to France. We felt a feeling of relief as we sailed off. We were away, and unless the car were to disintegrate nothing should stop us arriving in Colombo at the end of August. It did disintegrate a little but the expenses were under control. Dinner for seven with our parents the night before had cost us £14, while the fare for three passengers and our car from Lydd was £13. We had each contributed £500 to a kitty. Apart from a further £150 which we later had transferred from London, this was to suffice for our entire expedition, except for our final air fares home. Any personal expenditure was noted and by and by repaid to the kitty.

With a British skew, it might be imagined that the route to the Bosphorus and Istanbul from Calais is more south than east. Broadly, Istanbul is approximately 700 miles to our south and 1,400 miles to our east. It was south to Reims and Épernay, then turn left to Nancy and continue east to Strasbourg. We crossed the Rhine and took the Autobahn to Karlsruhe, skirting the Black Forest, and then a little more than 100 miles further we crossed the Danube at Ulm. We passed Munich to enter Austria at Salzburg, a city due east of Nancy. Then we went southwards to Klagenfurt and once more crossed the Austrian border via the notorious Loibl Pass into Yugoslavia (now Slovenia).

This was Robin's choice for crossing the Alps. "The Loibl is not the highest, but the steepest," Robin persuaded us, "and it will be good training for the Khyber." It was. We went over with a full load and eighteen gallons of petrol on board, the poor machine scraping the ground at every hairpin, and once we had to get out and push. We drove a total of 1,800 miles to Istanbul, covering over 800 miles on the last day.

These three "overnights" in Europe allowed us to shake down our camping and cooking arrangements. The first, in the forests that surround Nancy, was a perfect sylvan spot. This was a "dry camp", which is to say an unofficial camping ground as opposed to the great camping villages that were established all over Europe at that time with some amenities. The Casino tent looked magnificent when pitched and the mosquito net fitted perfectly too. We unscrewed and pulled the front seats out of the car. They made good dining chairs along with a folding camp stool. Our first effort with the pressure cooker was somewhat primitive but we looked forward to improving our technique.

We cruised between 60–75 mph on the Autobahn as far as Salzburg. The official camp in Salzburg had been recommended to us, as it had showers and shops selling fresh fruit and vegetables. We had a tastier dinner dining on steak and kidney pie. We met a man from Bristol who had been delivering shoes to refugees from Hungary as a holiday task. The next day we made better porridge but drove slower through the beautiful Austrian mountains.

The Yugoslav customs officers were unexpectedly easy, and so surprised were we at passing through so quickly that we forgot the "carnet" (an essential document at that time) and were twenty minutes down the road before Robin remembered it. When we reached Ljubljana we joined the Autocesta to Zagreb, where after some investigations of back streets and residential quarters we found the local camping sites, which again had showers and other amenities.

We were in Belgrade the following day, lunching at that excellent restaurant, the Café de Paris, discovered by Anthony Kenny and me at Easter. We went on to see Mike, the mechanic who had helped me on my last visit. He gave us such a painstaking service that we were late setting off. In our haste we were then stopped for speeding, paying a 400 dinar on-the-spot fine. It was nightfall by the time we reached the Nis campsite, where we had to be if we were to cross Bulgaria within the next day. We had to do this as we only had a twenty-four hour visa.

Bulgaria was fun. The customs procedures were lengthy but the officials were polite and even entertaining at times, pointing out photographs of Khrushchev with a smile and laughing at jokes about the "Big Four". Sofia was a drab and rather scruffy city on its outskirts but was reprieved as a European capital by some solid, square, Slavic institutional architecture in its centre. Particularly noticeable was the Hotel Balkan, the pride of Bulgarian tourism. But there were pinched faces and awful, cheap cosmetics, which the women seemed to treasure as a relief from everyday life. Not so in the countryside, where the people were contented and better off, profiting from the combine harvesters afforded by the collective farm system.

Until now, apart from the first night, we had used official camping grounds. In Istanbul we arrived at one o'clock in the morning at the downtown Ipek Palace

Hotel. We were awoken by the shouts of shoppers and merchants in the narrow street below, often interrupted by the "Aaark" bark of the street porters carrying wardrobes and cupboards full of goods on their backs. The cry was to warn pedestrians of their unstoppable momentum. Barrows did not exist and the streets were too narrow for motor vehicles. It was enchanting how East and West overlapped in that bifocal city.

Istanbul is as important as an oriental city as a Western one. Ankara, the capital, in Asia Minor, is the more westernised city of Turkey. Istanbul is significant in that it is the major European outpost of Islam and the old centre of the Ottoman Empire that stretched, in its prime, over the Balkans to the walls of Vienna. The Blue Mosque is built almost alongside the church of Hagia Sophia and the vision of the two together is a strong one full of self-confidence. Istanbul is also important to the Orient for its bazaar – its copper market, for example, was excellent. Even in India we were told that if we wanted to buy copper work then go to Istanbul; Isfahan for silver and Jaipur for jewellery, but Istanbul for copper and watches.

We visited a nightclub famous for its "cold drinks and hot dancing partners". A woman approached Robin and caressed his hand with the tips of her fingers. "What's she like, Robin?" we asked, our curiosity aroused. "Bloody sharp nails" was his pithy reply. This was the nature of Istanbul, sharp nails and all.

After a three night stay, we crossed the Bosphorus, took our last look at the sea – we would not see it again until Bombay – and drove up into the hills of Asia Minor. They were long and steep. We had now settled down to travelling in the car. Two sat in the front and the third seat, formed by sleeping bags in the rear, was more comfortable than we had expected – in fact, it was the best place for sleeping in the car. At night, we would stop shortly before dusk, pitch the tent, light the Tilley lamp (a paraffin lamp that gave a sharp white light) and prepare dinner. This was the big meal of the day, usually consisting of soup, then meat and vegetables and coffee. A pressure cooker was most useful for cooking the vegetables quickly and it also served to keep out sand, dust and other foreign objects. We had three tins of smoked salmon for special occasions. One night when we met two people at Persepolis we were able to invite them to a slap-up five-course dinner that we laid on. We never bored of Fray Bentos though.

We often had interested locals looking on while we cooked, and we would furnish them with coffee and cigarettes. There seemed to be a protocol for this in Eastern Turkey, where they would watch all our preparations but as soon as we began to eat they would go away. In India, nothing would move them but we found a technique in the end. The tactic was to go up to their leader (they always seemed to have one) and say "Good night" and "Goodbye" to him in a most friendly fashion. They would usually take the hint and leave us in peace.

Ankara still held many signs of the recent revolution, more than Istanbul where there was little trace of it bar frequent pictures of General Gürsel in the cafes and shop windows. In Ankara, a profusion of Turkish flags decorated government and many other buildings – we even saw one flying from a giant crane on a building site. Many troops were standing or strutting about the streets: when John asked for directions to the British Embassy, he was told: "Fork left after passing one policeman and two soldiers!" In both Ankara and Istanbul the inhabitants were avid newspaper readers – almost everyone was carrying a paper. New editions appeared frequently and were sold by numerous newspaper boys and at kiosks. The ill-feeling caused by the censorship of the press by the deposed Prime Minister Menderes helped his fall.

We crossed the Bosphorus by ferry – a wonderful way to appreciate the Istanbul skyline – and reached Scutari on the other side. After seventy miles we climbed to the Anatolian plateau that was to support us for 4,000 miles until the Punjab. This is not to mention the several mountain ranges that stand on this plateau that we had to negotiate. The temperature dropped. The diary for day 8 noted that John put his pyjamas on for the first time that evening.

After Ankara, the landscape changed. Westwards, Asia Minor is a fertile, populous land and it is not difficult to understand its attraction to ancient rulers who coveted its manpower and wealth. To the east of the capital, however, the land is barren, less populated and there are many signs of erosion. Throughout the rest of our journey through the Middle East, there was to be little change in the scenery: desert and scrub interrupted only by the occasional oasis in which there was always a settlement or town of some sort. Only as far across as the Punjab, or the foothills of the Hindu Kush in Afghanistan, did we return to the full greenery of fertile land.

I had never appreciated how far it was from Ankara to the Turco–Iranian border – it was nearly 1,000 miles and it took us almost four days. We were all itching to see Iran and it seemed that we were never going to get out of Turkey. We made only 100 miles on one day but the next was more successful when we travelled over 300 miles. At the end of it we found the most beautiful camping site in a dell, just beside a stream. In the morning we awoke to see small human shapes silhouetted by the sunlight against the tent. The diary reports: "Crawled out of the tent to find a whole lot of kids ready to watch our doings. Made themselves useful by filling the bucket at the stream for washing, also by helping to jack the car up when we discovered a slow puncture. After breakfast, they made a general nuisance of themselves while we packed up."

The road was now much rougher: Eastern Turkey is more mountainous so we could not travel as fast. We passed through the towns of Kayseri, Sivas and Erzincan; there were large detachments of troops in these towns. The town of Erzurum came as a climax to these military outposts; so vital a military post was it that all travellers were required to have a military escort as they passed through. It was the place from which President Kennedy agreed to remove his rockets in exchange for Soviet withdrawal from Cuba in 1962. We stopped to buy potatoes and French beans a few miles beforehand and met a Turkish officer who had been for a three month training course in Virginia so could speak English well. When we arrived at the town boundary the guard telephoned for an escort and after fifteen minutes an officer arrived in a jeep and led us into the main barracks in the centre of town. I went in to show our passports and was received politely; meanwhile, a senior officer came up to John and Robin and bid welcome to Erzurum. We were impressed by the courtesy shown within the military community. Once cleared, the escorting officer squeezed himself into the car and led us out of the town.

The next day a huge truck carrying a huge crane jammed itself under the superstructure of a bridge and blocked the road entirely. We could not ford the river – it was too deep. The only alternative route was round close by the Russian border. It was longer, and in all probability poorly surfaced or closed for military reasons. We did not want to take it. When we arrived at the bridge people were already trying to dismantle the top half of the crane so the truck could pass under the bridge. We decided to hop up and help. We couldn't let down the tyres as they were solid rubber. We worked for an hour and a half before it was decided that the truck was ready for a second attempt. This time it got further but jammed itself even more seriously under the superstructure. Release was going to take a week, we thought, so the Russian border road it had to be. During the delay we had suffered much criticism from the drivers directed at British Leyland Trucks. They told us that the Swedish Scania-Vabis had much better brakes and engines. We only heard bad things about the British automotive industry on our trip. Gresham Cooke, the MP for Newbury where Robin and John lived, took up these complaints on our return, but British poor automotive manufacture was endemic.

The border roads turned out to be better than we had expected with some really beautiful scenery. We drove through a gorge formed by the River Aras and then came out into open country and travelled alongside the river which formed part of the Russian border. We could see Russian soldiers in their watch towers on the opposite side, eyeing us through their powerful binoculars. What did they make of the Austin A40 bumping along, loaded to the extent of its springs? To the east, Mount Ararat rose in the background – the mythical resting place of Noah's Ark. This must be one of the most beautiful mountains in the world. As an extinct volcano, its grandeur is unhindered by foothills, and to see its snows from the heat of the desert provides a remarkable, almost uncanny contrast. At 16,853 feet it dominates the whole Armenian plateau and was within our view for over a hundred miles.

There must have been few strangers along that

the evening when, in despair, he books a room in the hotel. Then, miraculously, all customs difficulties are overcome. We booked beds in the hotel without further discussion.

We continued to have almost daily trouble with the U bolt until we reached Shiraz when a clever mechanic fitted a jeep U bolt, drilling larger holes in the chassis to do so. From then on fixing the leaf springs became habitual. John and Robin, practical mechanical men, became good at it. One hour forty minutes was their record. The companionship we received from those garagistes of the road meant that, to us, they were the saints of every nation east of the Bosphorus.

Iranian roads were awful and continuously corrugated. We were forced to cross Iran's 2,000 miles at an average speed of 25 mph. The corrugations could play remarkable tricks with the vehicle: sometimes, when the surface suddenly worsened, the car would be thrown broadside to the road and we would bounce along in a sideways motion. It was said that if a certain speed is reached the car will "leap" from one corrugation to another, so giving a smooth ride, but our car was both too heavy and too slow to do this. In any case, this is a dangerous game in Iran because sooner or later the car will hit a concealed irrigation ditch or gutter running across the road and fracture the back axle.

Iranian cities were more than compensation for the roads. The first was Tabriz, the capital of Azerbaijan province (as distinct from the present independent state) in northern Iran. The car was broken again by this time and we limped into a little garage we found off the main street. It was run by a German speaking Persian who had at least three gold teeth and was the headmaster of a local school. He employed an amusing bunch of mechanics who spent half an hour trying to push-start an old Hillman before they discovered there was no petrol in it. While they worked on our springs the manager entertained us with tea. Shortly, an English speaking friend of his appeared whose name we later learned was Ali Tobraki. He was a charming man and offered to show us around the town the next morning. When he found that we wanted to camp somewhere for the night he would not allow us to go anywhere else but Shahkoli, the local park, which had, he declared, the best climate in Iran.

But what an effort it was! Nobody was allowed to camp there without the permission of the governor, and the governor could not be found. But nothing was too much trouble. Ali, who had studied at the University of Michigan, finally obtained permission. Shahkoli was indeed a delightful place. Built as a holiday spot for the Shah at the beginning of the century, it surrounds a large artificial lake at the heart of which is a big summerhouse, now a restaurant.

We met Ali as arranged in the morning. He took us to the bazaar and introduced us to a few of the stall-keepers that he knew. He said that some stallholders were in fact extremely rich, even though they could not read or write. They never did anything with their money but just piled it in a corner or put it under the mattress – they would never take it to a bank. Quite naturally, adjacent to the bazaar was the caravanserai where until twenty or thirty years ago the camel caravans would come in carrying their merchandise. Now, although throughout the Middle East there are still many camels to be seen, almost everything is carried by trucks. The caravanserai did not only serve as a place to unload goods but there would also be accommodation for the camels and their

but we were not very successful. The head of the Austin agency was helpful and did what he could. The expert on springs, however, was away on holiday for two weeks and nobody else could fix them. In addition, the two days following our arrival were public holidays so work would be slow; obviously, we had not arrived at the right time. We left our car at a workshop in the suburbs in the hands of Mr Monti, the workshop manager. He was informative about the intricacies of Tehran and Iran and advised us to go over the high pass to the Caspian Sea. He asked me what I had studied at Cambridge. "History," I replied. "Iranian history?" I had to disappoint him.

We set off for the Caspian Sea, climbing over the 9,000 feet pass that separates it from Tehran. We then descended to 90 feet below sea level which is the level of the Caspian. We found a camping spot on the beach, pitched our tent, had dinner and went to sleep. The Englishman is an inveterate seaside fan, for even as we got up to have our (admittedly late) pre-breakfast bathe we heard English voices: two families from the British colony in Tehran had arrived for a day beside the sea. One family was the Webbers, whom we were to meet up with later in Tehran. When we packed to go a short while later we found, to our horror, that the clutch hydraulic pipe had broken. We could not move from the beach. John and Robin hitchhiked into the nearest village hoping to get the pipe brazed. A religious holiday was in full swing but with the help of a Persian boy they found a man who was persuaded to do something about it. His work was not good, however, because, when fitted, the pipe leaked hydraulic fluid again and John needed two hours under the car – and the help of a rubber washer cut from the car's rubberised flooring – before it would move again. We remained one more night by the Caspian and returned the following morning to Tehran and Mr Monti's garage, the clutch holding out just long enough for us to reach the top of the pass but no further. Driving clutchless in Tehran traffic drained the nerves!

Tehran was a relatively new town by Persian standards, having been the capital for less than two centuries. The previous capital was Isfahan and it was to this city that we now made our way. Isfahan was the residence of the Anglican bishop of Iran, Bishop Thompson, and we had been told that as soon as we arrived we should go and see him as he would tell us what to see in the town. We found out from Irantour where he lived.

We went to the bishop's house but he was engaged at a conference of the heads of the Christian churches in the Orient. Instead we met Miss Gaster, a remarkable woman who ran a school for blind children in Isfahan. It was a constant struggle to keep this school going and she had to rely a good deal on charity.

Many Persians were still indifferent to the fate of afflicted children, maintaining the biblical attitude that their suffering is due to the sins of their fathers and they are only fit to beg. Miss Gaster looked after between thirty and forty children with only one helper, Miss Kathleen Stewart, a young American girl from Baltimore. They had just moved into a new building and, for the moment, the future looked a little more settled. She was hospitable, and let us have a shower, gave us lunch and had us tell the story of our journey. When she heard that John had brought his bagpipes she insisted that he play them at the entertainment her school was giving that night for members of the conference. Unfortunately, when the time came, John found that the bag had shrivelled up in the heat and his ritual of pouring honey or syrup down the bag to loosen it took at least twenty-four hours to

dried in the back of the car for a couple of hours it was not so good. After lunch we had more trouble with our rear springs but pressed on. At last we drove around a mountain in the late afternoon and spread out before us was Persepolis (Takht-e-Jamshid). It is a marvel of ancient architecture by virtue of its size, its levels, its shape and its stance, seemingly in the middle of nowhere. But was it?

If, as the Persepolis Foundations claims, Darius the Great's empire stretched "from Sardia to the Indus", then the location of Persepolis was entirely strategic. Most of the great Persian cities form a rough diagonal south-easterly line: Tabriz, Tehran, Isfahan, Yazd, Persepolis, Shriaz. While they were protected from the west by the Zagros Mountains, any invading army from the north would proceed southwards, sacking these cities. They would receive a rude shock, however, when they rounded a mountain to find Persepolis 500 yards before them, whereas Persian sentinels from atop the escarpment would have long espied them.

Equally, any enemy army approaching from the Indus across the southern desert would have been greatly fatigued and observed approaching from many miles away. Used as a fortress as well as a palace, a host of troops could be held at Persepolis and supplied from Shiraz, a few miles away.

No army could conquer Persia without first capturing Persepolis. This must have been why Alexander the Great burnt it down and sought to rule Persia with his satraps (regional proconsuls). The strategy was not only to deter any invader but also to dominate the people, the subordinate tribes and wild animals.

As well as strategic triumph, Persepolis is all about dominance. The complex bas reliefs flanking the huge

Apadana staircase entrance bear witness to that. They depict representatives from all over the stretch of this Eastern Empire bringing gifts to the great king, Darius the Great, and his successors. They show, for example, Ethiopians bringing a giraffe, people from the east with a bull, Indians from Sind (north-west India) with an ass, Parthians with a Bactrian camel carrying metal objects, Cappadocians leading horses, Assyrians with sheep, Armenians with a horse and double handed ewer, Elamite archers with a lioness and many others.

All the bas reliefs were sculpted with breathtaking skill. We met a Swedish archaeologist determined to prove that Greek artisans were involved. It has since been proved that they were, since evidence of the use of a Greek sculpting tool has been discovered. This is natural enough: persons of skill will always wander long distance to find work wherever it is offered.

It was a frontier and a palace. And huge – the size of a shopping centre. Like many European cathedrals it was built continuously over the centuries. It was still unfinished when Alexander attacked and burnt it in 330 BC. If he was to rule the world it could not be allowed to survive.

Camping by Persepolis was a privileged experience. When we passed there were no restrictions. It was here that we met two English hitchhikers whom we had first seen at the border coming into Iran. We had a memorable dinner party with them. We sat swapping experiences before they went off to their beds at the local tea shop to sleep, as they had dined in the spirit of the Ancients. The next night we camped at Persepolis again. During the day, we had been to Shiraz, thirty miles away, to mend our suspension again, this time much more effectively with the use of Jeep U bolts which held for the rest of

to nil and sent the oil thermometer off the gauge. We had to halt a while before things calmed. It was not until siesta time that we reached the border. It was half an hour before a stern-faced official appeared to deal with us. We were longer at the police and passport department which attached great importance to the "London" stamp in our passports, and when they had found them wrote screeds of Farsi in the visa section. We drove away to be stopped half a mile later at a military post where two soldiers and three children demanded our passports, then inspected them upside down; English looked more like Farsi (the Iranian language) that way up.

IV

Northwest Frontiers

The Pakistani customs post was seventy miles on inside the border at Nok Kundi. The road surface had changed as soon as we were across the border. It was not asphalt for the first twenty miles but there were no more corrugations, and what a relief that was. There was literally no traffic whatsoever, and all we passed was a military post and one or two shacks where people seemed to be living in the middle of nowhere; how they existed we could not imagine. This was the Baluchistan area of Pakistan and the colour of the sand had changed to an ashen hue, with forbidding mountains huge lumps of rock rising out of the plateau on either side. It was dark when we reached the customs post and if any place could qualify for being the ends of the earth, Nok Kundi must be on the shortlist. The area produced almost nothing of its own and all supplies had to be brought in by train or truck. We signed the entry book only to find that we were the first vehicle through for two days and the previous entry was Commander Saaed of the Pakistan Navy, whom we had met at the Turco–Iranian border. I can remember him telling us that he had no hostility against the Indian Navy, but when invited aboard one of their ships he had drunk much of their gin.

The customs officer told us to go first and have a meal

at the rest house. We knew we were in India as he had a punkah-wallah (a man to work the fan to keep him cool) so we confidently ordered chicken curry. There was no demur but no chicken either. The problem was, to say so would have had him lose face. We should have had more sense and the tact to change our order in the first place, but it was now too late. Two hours later there was a squawk. A chicken had been found but it took another two hours to pluck and cook it. It was now midnight by Pakistan time (an hour and a quarter ahead of Iranian time), so by the time we were ready to return to customs we had to get the officer out of bed. The customs officer was a little grumpy about it all but the passport officer had brought his punkah-wallah with him again to cool him while he worked. When we apologised for disturbing him he humbly said: "All right, sire, it's my duty, please," as the punkah-wallah creaked in the background.

Perhaps because of the chicken or bad water at the rest house, the next day John was feeling very ill. He sat in the back of the car for the 300 mile trip across Baluchistan to Quetta. Our own water in the car was as warm as a cup of tea. We stopped at a rest house on the way to pick up a reserve of water in case we broke down and could not make Quetta that day.

Forty miles from Quetta the engine stopped on a hill. John roused himself, rightly suspecting that the carburettor jet had bunged up with dust, and managed to clear it. At last in Quetta, we put up at the Hotel Chiltan and went straight off to have a beer to celebrate "getting across". It was 6,000 miles and almost a month since we had left England. The beer was called London Lager, Nelson Brand (complete with a picture of the column) and was made in Rawalpindi. We were very pleased with the way things had gone because, despite breakdowns, we were ahead of the rather conservative schedule we had planned. Consequently, we had begun to have all sorts of wild ideas like including Kashmir, Kathmandu or Calcutta (Kolkata) in the itinerary.

Quetta was largely destroyed in 1935 by a disastrous earthquake when 23,000 people were killed. We were amazed by the British influences we had seen, although later we were to grow accustomed to it. I wrote home at that time: "The British influence is quite fantastic, they could have left yesterday." The sign came when we crossed the border and the railway begins. Water tenders lying in sidings with 'Water tanker. Not to be loose shunted' written on them come as rather a surprise after coming so far. Then the notice, 'Left drive in Pakistan'. The rest houses we passed on the desert road had notices saying 'Knock for help' outside, all these notices in English. Then came Quetta, where it really hits you. It is a hill station with a pleasant climate which also has important strategic significance, guarding the Bolan Pass to the south and the Khojak Pass to Kandahar in Afghanistan to the north. In the town, the road names were unchanged: Pretoria Road, Mafeking Road and Kimberley Road were all there still. The old barrack blocks still stood, old cannons ornamented them as relics of military greatness. The British Indian Army had its staff college there. The residency was still called the Residency, the GOC's House still the GOC's House. The golf links were still used. The standard of service we received both in the hotel and elsewhere was unequalled. Willing, unquestioning, uncomplaining. Later we were to see some great British achievements both in India and Pakistan, such as the engineering feats involved in building the bridges and tunnels of the North Western State Railway and the grand architectural achievement of New Delhi.

We had a restful two day stay in Quetta, relaxing with the service of the hotel. The first morning the room boy came in with tea, a few minutes later the barber arrived and after him the laundry man. That morning we met two undergraduates from the University of Toronto, one Canadian and the other English. They had driven out from England in a Land Rover, had been to Afghanistan and were now on their way back west to stay with some friends in Beirut. They were able to give us some helpful advice on what to do in Afghanistan and we were able to tell them about the southern Persia route, as they had come out by Mashhad and driven north of the desert into Herat, Afghanistan. They told us to join the Afghan International Club in Kabul, to avoid Afghan bread since it seemed to have grit in it but on no account to miss the cottage machine gun industry near Peshawar. All this turned out to be good advice. They too had experienced the nocturnal contrasts of well served hotels and roadside dry camping.

After driving through the spectacular scenery of the 7,500 foot Khojak Pass we encountered little trouble in entering Afghanistan. We discovered later that this was through the efforts of Mr. Tarzi, chief of Afghantour who was doing so much to increase the country's tourist trade. The officials merely stamped our passports and didn't even bother to look at the triptyque for the car. Much of the Afghan scenery was as I had imagined it to be through reading Kipling's *Ballad of East and West*: "There is rock to the left, and rock to the right, and low lean thorn between" – such was the descriptive genius of the poet. Barren land with rocky outcrops and, in the distance, a backdrop of mountains. The Afghans themselves are a fine-looking race of people with a very proud bearing. As it happened, the road to Kandahar ran parallel with the eastern provincial border of Helmand Province which, fifty years later, British troops fought so hard to keep from the Taliban.

There was a good road into Kandahar but when we turned north-east to drive to Kabul, not only did the asphalt disappear but so did the road – as one traveller put it: "There were big enough holes for the car to fall into." But it gradually improved and on some stretches we reached 35–40 mph. Most of the bridges were washed away so we had to descend to the (usually dry) river beds. Reaching Kabul, we followed the advice that we had been given, joined the International Club and lunched with Kabul's international set. We picked up some of the gossip: two years ago there was hardly a street paved in the city. Then the Russians moved in and paved the main streets as well as many of the minor ones. The Americans and Russians vied with one another for supremacy and who could provide the most aid to gain the favour of the Afghan government.

Afghanistan has acted as a buffer state between Pakistan and Russia. Thus derives its politico-geographic importance. The United States had built a road outside the city and had also contributed a good deal to the expansion of the University of Kabul but, according to US sources in Kabul, the Russians had the upper hand and only allowed the Americans to continue their aid programme to save themselves money for when they presumed to move in for good, in four or five years' time.

To me, all this took no account of the Afghans themselves who are a highly independent people with a way of maintaining their independence through deft diplomacy. At that time they were maintaining a clever balance between the two powers and profiting from them both; they had no cause to be rid of either, even if they had more sympathy with Russia. Their country is mountainous and hard to control

We visited the British embassy. This was a fine residence built outside the city. We met the ambassador and defence attaché. The latter wanted to know if we had seen any Russian tanks on our way. We had not. The very question gave us a jolt for we had seen no sign of an impending Russian incursion, although this developed into invasion some years later. The defence attaché must have had his ear very near to the ground.

We spent but one night in Kabul before moving off on an excursion initiated by Robin to the foothills of the Hindu Kush by the valleys of Bamiyan and Band-i-Amir. Despite the terrible roads, this was one of the more beautiful drives we took. We drove through the gorge where Genghis Khan and his Mongol hordes had passed in the thirteenth century. They and other invaders have left their mark, for in the villages the flat, Mongol features are much in evidence. Shortly before we reached Bamiyan itself, we passed the Red City, an ancient town cut high in the red rock of the area. Bamiyan is the site of an ancient Buddhist civilisation founded in the fourth century. Cut into the solid rock of the cliff which overshadows the village are two great Buddhas. One is 172 feet high and the other 115 feet (for comparison, Nelson's column in Trafalgar Square is 169 feet high). It is possible to climb up inside the cliff by way of interior staircases to the heads of the statues. Not only the priests but also the people of the settlement itself lived in caves cut out of the rock. The Buddhas have been attacked many times over the centuries, but it was the Taliban who finally dynamited and destroyed the carved rock statues cleft in the cliff some forty years after our visit.

We made friends in the village with the teashop man,

who gave us a lunch of rice and meat laid out in front of us while we sat, cross-legged, on the floor. We had tea too, which is a safe drink to buy in the East as you know that the water has been boiled. Typically, the ritual is that you are offered a choice in the variety of tea – for example, green tea or the more normal brown variety. Near Peshawar they were very proud of their green tea. Then the boiling water is poured out of a giant samovar into a small teapot, and usually each person receives a separate pot. If you want sugar it falls to the bottom of the cup, which normally is not stirred but just absorbed into the tea; this usually means that there is enough left at the bottom for a second cup.

The next day we moved up over worse roads to the natural lakes and dams of Band-i-Amir. These three lakes, very deep and very blue, are bounded at one end by natural barrages. They are very like the reservoirs adjacent to London Heathrow. We had a swim but the water (which is supposed to cure all diseases) was so cold that we soon got out. Whatever the curative properties of those waters they seemed to be of little use to John and me, for that night we both had a go of what we later discovered to be KTs (Kabul Trots).

On the first night of our arrival in Kabul, we had met Don Holmes, a delightful Nova-Scotian who was working for the International Cooperation Administration, an American aid programme. He offered typical North American hospitality. He had invited us to go and stay with him when we returned to Kabul: "In three days' time? Good, I'll organise a party. Give me a call when you get back. My house is the only one with salmon squares in the wall. No bell, just pound on the door!" When we returned to Kabul we telephoned him through the efficient automatic system they had there and he had organised everything. The party was first rate: Martinis, French wine, liqueurs and a cold buffet. He had bought everything, except the ham, in the local bazaar. We could hardly believe we were in Kabul. Also at the party were two others who were passing through Kabul but they were on their way to Moscow, going to the International Conference of Orientalists. They were waiting in Kabul, becoming more angry with the Russian airline, Aeroflot, who had cancelled their booking. We arranged to meet up the next day and visit the Kabul Museum.

We had the car under repair at the time so we took one of Kabul's Russian taxis, since the museum stood at the end of a long boulevard that led out of the centre of town towards the palace. The boulevard was built by King Amanullah around 1930 as one of his efforts to westernise Afghanistan. The museum derives much of its interest from the Greco-Buddhist relics that are to be found there. There seemed to be tremendous Greek influence on the early artwork in Afghanistan, and this influence appeared before the invasion of Alexander the Great. We saw a sculpture of a Buddha that was extremely similar to the classical Western likeness of Christ. Was this where and when two cultures had met? The exchange of labour between Greek, Arabic and Persian cultures may stretch back over many unwritten centuries. Surely, much communication will have taken place, as it ever has, through itinerant skilled craftsmen walking to where the work is and sharpening their skills together.

The next day we left for Pakistan again, travelling though Jalalabad towards the Khyber Pass. The road much improved after Jalalabad and we rocketed along at nearly 70 mph. The Khyber has been a disappointment to many but we did not find it so. It may not be as steep as the Loibl Pass, and the fact that the road was asphalt

Mount Ararat

The Ancient eastern world found its benchmarks in a mixture of myth and fact. So it may have been that Noah's flood was the Black Sea, once an inland lake, bursting its banks before finding its outlet through the Dardanelles. So where, thought the ancients, would his Ark come to rest? Why, Mount Ararat of course, an isolated, snow capped extinct volcano visible for a hundred miles around. Thus its mythical significance and dominating quality. What a story!

Sunset.

Mount Ararat towers over Dogubayazit.

Ararat as background as we take our first Iranian fuel at 10p a gallon.

Persepolis

Despite excavations since 1931, when we arrived in 1960, Persepolis seemed little changed since Alexander had plundered and left it. Yet the messages were as clear as when Darius I had created them around 500 BC. He knew the empire he had made and how to sustain it. Conquering lands from the Indus to the Balkans, asserting laws, he introduced a system of weights and measures. He claimed the submission of twenty-three peoples, centring his power on strategic Persepolis. He illustrated this by bas reliefs (detailed to cuticles of fingernails) of their submission by delegates, each bringing gifts representative of their land, and his superiority over legendary wild animals by slaying them.

Naqsh-e Rustam

Two miles from Persepolis. A vast perpendicular rock face in which is contained the remains of at least four Persian kings including Darius I and Xerxes I. To the left is the rock relief of the Roman Emperor Valerian paying homage to the Sassanian King Shapur I after being defeated by him in 260 AD.

Islamic Architecture

When it comes to Islamic architecture, "colour, colour, colour," is the theme, and it all looks so modern.

Golestan Palace in Tehran, Iran, former residence of the Shah.

Humayun's Tomb, Delhi, India.

Badshahi Mosque, Lahore, Pakistan, one of the largest mosques in Islam.

Masjed-e-Sheikh Lotfallah Mosque, Isfahan, Iran.

The Shalimar Gardens, Lahore, Pakistan.

The music hall in the Ali Qapu Palace, Isfahan, Iran. The musicians would play, then exit. Enter the Shah, and the music would play back.

Hagia Sophia, Istanbul, Turkey.

The Taj Mahal, India.

Hagia Sofia, Istanbul.

Sultan Ahmed Mosque
(Blue Mosque), Istanbul.

may disturb the mystique, but no traveller can fail to be impressed by its drama and strategic importance. It was still heavily fortified – most of the installations were built by the British – with control posts manned by men of the Khyber Rifles, while the area itself was inhabited by armed tribesmen who stood and sat by the roadside. We were delayed for one-and-a-half hours by the Pakistan customs.

We spent the following two nights in the government dak bungalow; dak bungalows and government rest houses were often our havens of value and shelter in both Pakistan and India, providing cheap accommodation in countries where camping spots were hard to find because of monsoon flooding and blanket cultivation. Generally, they were established under British rule to house tax collectors and other government administration officers.

The first morning we were awakened by a government guide we had met the night before and a friend of his, the Chief of Police in Peshawar. He wanted to talk of England which he had visited on an eight week course three years before. We chatted to him in our pyjamas for an hour, then he invited us to tea. Our guide had promised us that he would take us to visit the cottage gun industry that we had been recommended to see by our two friends in Quetta. We set off after breakfast, and ten miles south of Peshawar we entered the tribal area of the Kohat Pass which had not yet come under government jurisdiction. Our guide told us, "When the British were here they used to rebel against the government, but now they are more civilised and fight only amongst themselves."

We soon arrived at the centre of the industry, the village of Dogbat near Kohat, a town of 80,000 people. These tribal areas are significant. We went into one of the shops which sold weapons and we were offered a Lee–

Enfield service rifle for 200 rupees (£17), while a Mauser cost 350 rupees. The village chief conducted us through the various workshops. All the lathes were worked by hand, although they were hoping for an electricity supply in the near future. We saw them rounding and drilling the barrels and then they showed us the ingenious tool they used for the rifling process. It was remarkable how they were able to manufacture these complicated pieces of machinery with such primitive equipment. In another shop there were men employed cutting bolts, bolt casings and pistols from solid chunks of steel; others were fashioning the woodwork for the rifles. The finished articles seemed remarkably sound and some of the bolt actions that we tested seemed as good as any service rifle. When, at last, all is ready for assembly, the number, the brand name and the year of manufacture is stamped on the gun. "Made in England" or "Made in Germany", according to the country of the prototype, is also inscribed – and in the case of the Lee–Enfield the crown logo is not forgotten.

We spoke about the industry with the chief's son, who was at that time on vacation from university in Peshawar. "We can make all the weapons of all the governments," he declared. "It is a craft given to us by our forefathers who began making guns at the time of the Free War against the British." (He was referring to the Indian Rebellion of 1857.) He was reading politics and economics and later hoped to go to Oxford to study. He denied that he was going to open a branch of the family trade there, but he planned to return home to Dogbat to work in the trade.

They made ammunition too. We entered the ammunition shop were people were filling brass cartridge cases with gunpowder and inserting the bullets on top. They claim never to have accidents since they are so careful. The guns are bought by the tribesmen themselves (and this is not the only tribal area in Pakistan) and many are smuggled out to controlled parts of Pakistan and into Afghanistan. Nobody seems to consider frontier controls as any great problem. In fact, since the frontiers are so long and in most cases so deserted, it is little trouble to drive a camel caravan over the border whether loaded with arms or opium. The trouble (and the law) comes when the goods reach the towns for distribution. Neither is there any control of poppy growing in the tribal areas, and thus much opium still reaches India.

Tea that afternoon, back in Peshawar with the chief of police, was a treat. A monumental repast was laid out for us, with all the fruits of the East – mangoes, peaches, plums – and after that some exotic cakes. The local irrigation officer was also invited. He was an interesting man who had spent eight months travelling through Europe. Absent at first was our host's wife who was observing purdah. She appeared for a brief greeting. Also there was a Pashtu poet with whom it was difficult to have much conversation but to whom we were sure to offer great respect.

Peshawar itself, like many Indian military towns, was divided into two areas: the town and the cantonment. The well-to-do lived in the cantonment, while the bazaar and most of the shops were in the town. Peshawar was much more like the typical Indian town that I had always imagined, with the bazaars situated in higgledy-piggledy streets and rickety buildings three to five storeys high. Down below we mingled with the people, the shouting, the cows and the donkeys.

We left at lunchtime the next day and after two hours crossed the Indus and passed through Rawalpindi. We stopped off in Lahore where we picked up the rest of our baggage, which we had forwarded to Quetta through the good offices of the National and Grindlays Bank. Robin had an introduction to the firm which had branches throughout Pakistan, India, East Africa and Rhodesia. They were a great help throughout this part of the trip. We met an Englishman in Lahore who had stayed on after the British had moved out. He had been in the Orient for forty years. "The first seven years are the worst," grunted Mr Talbot (for that was his name). He had no great love for either Clement Attlee or Earl Mountbatten, thinking their 1947 policy of Partition of India entirely misguided. He spoke with a passion and a view typical of a large number of British expats in India and Pakistan. It was indeed a terrible and murderous time. Behind his fearsome opinion, which of course bears truth, is the idea that the British never had to leave.

I quote it below as I wrote it that evening. Mr Talbot told of the riots and the murder that went on at that time. It is often forgotten, or hardly known, that between one and two million people died as a result of the disturbances caused by the partition of 1947/8. He felt strongly and spoke it. He started with Kashmir: in the Mountbatten/ Radcliffe Partition it had been given to India rather than Pakistan, despite it being mainly Muslim, yet India itself is the largest Muslim country in the world. He expounded:

> In the old days, you could drive up to
> Srinagar, the capital of Kashmir, 250 miles,
> just for a meal or weekend. But that was in
> the good old days. Then came that arch-
> criminal Clement Attlee and his minion
> Battenberg – I refuse to call him by his
> assumed name. They finished it all. Kashmir
> was a Muslim state ruled by a Hindu. No

Englishman could interfere with that – what could the British know of such a situation? The commissioner here, Jenkins, flew four times to Delhi to tell Battenberg that if he carried through his policy he would be responsible for the loss of more lives than he ever was in the Second World War.

It was true. I came out of the garage on 14 June 1947 and saw by the petrol pumps over there, the two attendants lying dead in a pool of blood, stabbed. On 17 June 1947 I had a letter I needed to post and I went down to the railway station. It was full of the dead and dying.

One Sikh was lying as though in the midst of a surgical operation. But he was still living. He gasped "Water" as I went by. As I looked round for where it was, a Muslim came up to me and warned that I should suffer in the same way if I helped the Sikh.

It was a terrible experience. The British did give these people peace; they gave them nothing else, but they did give them peace. All the rest, the people paid for – paid through the nose for with good money. The British who ran the railways got a better income out here than they ever would have for the same jobs back home. Some of them were wasters, I know.

At an ordnance depot that I was at during the war, 2,000 people broke into a riot. The statistics looked ugly. The Riot Act was read, nobody heard it. The order was given and five rounds were fired. A few men were killed. The riot broke up at once. The British gave peace.

Once in a village a man told me, "I wish the British were back."

"What's this, a bit of flattery?" I asked.

"No, but if you gave a British sahib a bottle of whisky to do something, he will do it. If you give an Indian sahib 500 rupees to do something, he may not."

At the time the Pakistanis were trying to push Mr Talbot out of his job. He ran one of the garages out of Lahore, could speak fluent Urdu and had a great love for the people. Another man joined us. He ran a brass shop. He accused the British of "running away". We retreated, punch drunk.

Arguments, deeply felt, over the partition and independence of India continue seventy years on. They are as deeply felt and will never be settled. The circumstances caused much agony and more than a million deaths.

After all this criticism of the British, we recovered the car from its repair and ourselves with a drink at Faletti's, the swell hotel at that time.

The next day was spent with a wonderful man who signed himself on as our guide with expressions of "international brotherhood", of wanting to meet Cambridge people and so on. He came to our room after breakfast and, after returning the car to Kandawalla Motors as the oil leak persisted, we took a "tonga" (horse cab) with him to the fort and spent two hours looking round. We had a stop for sherbet – the Indian answer to Coca Cola – and then met him again at five o'clock. We went to the Badshahi Mosque, a huge but beautiful building and the largest mosque in the Islamic world. We were permitted to climb a minaret for a fine view of Lahore. This is a huge city, the thirty-second largest in the world with a population of ten million. It stands near the Indian border and the banks of the Ravi River, a tributary of the Indus. It had fantastic jewels inlaid into marble and the effect was exceptional.

Jahangir's tomb was next which lay outside the city. On the other side of town were the Shalimar Gardens which were arranged in three enormous terraces. "Small" was obviously not a word used much in this remarkable and friendly city where people travel habitually holding hands in tongas.

We changed £5 with the brass shop manager at a good rate, then took our guide to dinner and the movies. We saw *It Started with a Kiss* starring Debbie Reynolds and Glenn Ford, parting with our guide at quarter to twelve. The following day we attended Anglican Communion in the impressive red brick cathedral and departed for the Indian frontier.

Lahore is not far from the Indian border. We arrived at the customs post, "Attock Cross Roads", on 31 July. It was an irritating border stop as it was three hours before we were able to pass through. The Indians have certainly inherited the bureaucratic habit from the British because most of this period was occupied by form filling. I complained to the official that we had been kept waiting for two hours. "You will be here for one hour more," was his reply. At last we were free.

V

Kashmir

The Indian sub-continent is host to a number of quite different but equally intense religions. Lahore in Pakistan, which we had just left, is one of the ten largest Islamic cities in the world. Yet just forty miles away, albeit across the border into India, is Amritsar – the home of the Golden Temple, the sacred shrine of the Sikh religion.

We stopped in Amritsar to visit the Golden Temple. Many have found this more enthralling than the Taj Mahal, but the two are vastly different – for one thing the temple is a centre of worship and the other a mausoleum. While the Taj Mahal is in the midst of a great park, the Golden Temple is hidden among scruffy narrow streets in the centre of the town. "Go to the main square and turn left at the statue of Queen Victoria," we were told. Certainly, a most fetching statue of the queen as a young woman was to be found at its entrance.

The unprepossessing appearance of the building from the outside contrasts with the dazzling beauty and splendour of the interior and the temple grounds. This is the sort of surprise that the East often springs upon the Western traveller: in the midst of squalor, poverty and ugliness they throw up a gem that is quite breathtaking in its brilliance and more so on account of its impoverished surroundings. The unexpectedness of the glory contributes to its wonder.

The Golden Temple itself is set in the middle of a large square pool and its gold roof reflects on the water. This sight hits the eye on passing through the main gate. Access to the temple is gained by a paved causeway. We were taken first to the kitchens and eating house where every visitor, no matter what his religion, may be fed free of charge. All the cooks and workers there were volunteers and we watched them baking chapattis by the dozen for the evening meal. Many others were bathing in the pool to take advantage of its holy properties. Whole families had been brought to dip in the waters.

We passed a group of about fifty who were sitting and talking cheerfully amongst themselves. We were told that they confidently expected to spend that night in jail. They were taking part in the movement against the government to form a separate Punjabi speaking state. This virtually means a Sikh state six million strong. Every night some of them would demonstrate in the streets of Amritsar and many of them would be locked up. This was all to the good, they believed, for if they were in jail, the government would have to feed them and keep them. If enough of them were locked up they would cost the government so much money that they would be forced to grant them their wishes. At that time, over 20,000 had been arrested according to a notice that hung on a wall, rather in the way that enthusiastic industrialists display the production figures of the previous period.

Inside the temple, the holy of holies itself, a good deal was going on. In the middle was a large lake with a causeway leading to a small island of two stories. On the ground floor there was a group of musicians and chanters who were playing while a group alongside the lake sat and watched. Upstairs there were two men reading the Guru

Granth Sahib out loud during the day and night. It was said that by taking shifts, the entire book of 1,430 pages (angs) was read through every twenty-four hours. It is the central religious scripture of Sikhism.

We turned north to Kashmir from Amritsar. Partition prevented us using the old, shorter (and allegedly much better) road across the Indo–Pakistani border, turning off at Rawalpindi (affectionately known as "Pindi") and driving through Murree. We turned off at Jammu, beyond which the surface was still poor, and it is a two day drive as opposed to an afternoon's drive from Rawalpindi and Kashmir – once a place for a quiet weekend. But Kashmir, as Mr Talbot had described, belonged to India so this way was barred. On the way up we stopped at a control point to pay a toll for the upkeep of the road. There was a weighbridge there so we took the opportunity of weighing the car – the result was 26 cwt without us aboard which meant that the car was normally carrying its own weight again. We were still chuckling over this discovery when a glance at the rear spring showed the main leaf to be broken. The glance would most certainly come from the eyes of Robin or John without whose mechanical instincts and knowledge we could not have progressed at all.

We laboured on to Jumna, sixty miles away, and here we were fortunate enough to find Mr Saram, BA. He was the manager of the government garage there and helped us out, only charging us for two new leaves for the spring. This was the third garage in a row which had given us free service, as there had been one in Kabul and Mr Talbot in Lahore before this. We met with great generosity in these parts and huge friendship too.

That night we stayed in the dak bungalow in the village of Kud, 6,000 feet up in the hills. It had been tiring driving from Jumna which we had left about two hours before at twenty past five. The road had become much more twisty and had narrowed. It was crowded with large Mercedes trucks of which, we learned later, nearly 500 left Jumna daily for the Vale of Kashmir. Mostly they were painted in psychedelic colours redolent of the Hindu faith. They were difficult to overtake for such was the din inside the driver's cab that they could rarely hear your horn. Once they did the drivers were courteous, immediately pulling into the side and stopping to let you pass, even if it meant losing carefully conserved revs in the middle of a steep hill. If we were lucky, the truck would have a passenger on the back who would bang on the roof of the cab to inform the driver of our presence. This goes on all over the Middle East and Orient. It can be quite dangerous on a dirt road when trucks blow up a thick blanket of dust which prevents the driver following the truck from seeing what is coming the other way, even if there is a chance to pass, yet having to follow close behind to give the truck a better chance of hearing the horn.

Fortunately, except where repairs were going on, the road to Kashmir was asphalt and we did not have this difficulty. But it was steep and narrow for lorries. They were usually in low gear which made the din inside their cabs even greater. Much to our chagrin, most of these trucks were Mercedes-Benz – the chassis was made under licence in India and then driven to distribution centres throughout the country. The eventual owners themselves would very often build the wooden body onto them, but if they did not do this they would certainly decorate them. Some of the trucks looked extremely attractive, painted all over with brightly coloured landscapes or religious designs. Whatever the decoration, the tailboards of the trucks would invariably have, often in ornate lettering, the inscription, "Horn please", and an arrow pointing towards the driving cabin. British manufacturers had no idea of reliability standards in these parts. If they did, then they did not want to know. They were in denial, and there was no evidence of any attempt to recapture the old imperial automotive markets. The Hindustan Ambassador, a replica of the old Morris Oxford, was produced in India; from what we saw, it seemed to survive the roads.

Another heavy road user in those parts was the army which moved up and down this picturesque road in long convoys. It would sometimes take an hour or more to pass one, or longer if we happened to come across some roadworks, of which there were several. But delays on the road were not always caused by roadworks or other traffic overtaking. Often, when we were brought to a halt behind a line of traffic it was best to get out and walk on ahead to discover what the trouble was and help to sort it out. We had done this, albeit unsuccessfully, when the crane was stuck under the bridge in Turkey. Truckers the world over, are delighted to have the monotony of their work broken by some little contretemps on the road. When it occurs they like to make quite an event out of it, often ignoring the obvious way out of the difficulty, to take advantage of the opportunity for a discussion.

An unusual obstacle presented itself on the way to Jammu in the form of a Sunday protest march. The entire population of a local village – men, women and children – were marching in the road and refusing to let any traffic through. We drove up behind them and Robin and I hopped out to see what all the fuss was about. It appeared that the government had taken their money in taxation and had given them little in return. Surrounding villages had been given electric power but they had not.

Furthermore, they still had to walk three miles to their nearest water supply. We offered our sympathies and became quite friendly, but this was not sufficient for us to pass through this determined procession. Meanwhile, John was being sued, out of court, for damages by a man who claimed he'd had his foot run over by the Austin. He seemed to be little the worse for it and John managed to talk him round.

We followed the protest for about half an hour and were beginning to wonder how we were to get through them, for there seemed to be little possibility of them taking a lunch break or anything of that sort. But after a little time in India you learn not to worry, for everything comes right in the end. We came across a double Bailey bridge which operated as a dual carriageway. Like many bridges on that road it had a military guard, and the intelligent sergeant steered the procession up the left side and signalled us to pass up the other.

Such was the hectic road to Kashmir. It was dark when we stopped outside the dak bungalow at the village of Kud, halfway to Srinagar and 6,000 feet up in the foothills of the Hindu Kush. Since two busloads of people were already in occupation we were apprehensive of our chances of finding accommodation. Again, everything always turns out all right in India. On first enquiring the place seemed to be full, so we sought out the manager who appeared from the kitchens. When we had presented him with our problem, he thought a little, made up his mind and led us down the hill, across the road and down the hill again to another bungalow, outside of which some passengers from the bus were squatting cooking their chapattis and curry. He pushed through them and showed us a bare and empty room which we could have all to ourselves for cooking and setting up our camp beds.

We readily accepted his offer. He called two porters to bring down our baggage. Problem solved.

The buses left early the next morning. We were awoken by the clatter of the passengers' departure. We made an early exit ourselves and rolled into Srinagar, the summer capital of Kashmir, a little before two o'clock that afternoon. The city industry was the renting of houseboats on the nearby Dal Lake. We had barely reached the outskirts when we were stopped by two houseboatmen who were determined that they should be the first to offer their houseboat for hire during our sojourn in the area. Now, we had read about the exotic life that was to be had aboard a houseboat in Kashmir and, if the price was reasonable, we were resolved to try it. We had imagined that it would be far beyond our budget.

When these houseboatmen began to talk about thirty rupees (£2) a day all in for the three of us, our hopes began to rise, but we had learned enough about tourism to know that it is imprudent to accept the first attractive offer one receives, but to mull it over, confident that a better offer will be presented soon enough by someone else. True to a routine that we had established for ourselves – which was when we arrived at a new place to go and have lunch at the best hotel in town and decide what to do with the rest of our stay from there – we made for the Oberoi Palace Hotel, which was the converted palace of the maharajah of Kashmir who was no longer allowed to visit the district.

Ignoring the shouts and gesticulations of other would-be houseboat hosts, we drove there for an excellent lunch, exquisitely served while we sat, a little embarrassed, in our best sports shirts. After lunch the man in the hotel tourist office told us of government approved houseboats with a fixed price of thirty rupees; we didn't like the sound of these at all so we went out to revisit the open market.

As we expected, no sooner were we out of the hotel grounds and on the road that ran alongside the placid, mirror-like Dal Lake on which many of the houseboats floated, than we were surrounded by a horde. They shouted and banged on the car, and inside sixty seconds we were told of the virtues of a score of different vessels. Just when we had decided that this was more than we could tolerate and were about to drive on, Robin was impressed by a man with a somewhat quieter approach who was able to produce an exotic picture of his craft.

To the jeers and disappointed shouts of the others, we allowed this man to climb in beside us. He directed us to a little quay at the side of the lake to which were tied small boats called shikaras. These have an appearance not unlike that of gondolas and are propelled by means of spade-like paddles.

Shikaras were not only privately owned but also hired out as taxis to convey people from the mainland to the houseboats or, as the Dal Lake stretched that far, into the very centre of Srinagar. The pride of many of these taxis was having full spring seats. Furthermore, each taxi had a name, often an extraordinary one. These two pieces of information were displayed on a signboard affixed to the roof. The combination of the two brought about some rather remarkable results. One shikara was called "King Kong" and the sign read "'King Kong' On Full Spring Seats". Some were even funnier like, "'Here Am I But Where Are You' On Full Spring Seats'", but the funniest one was, "'Doings' On Full Spring Seats'".

We stepped aboard one of these extraordinary craft and, in the luxury of full spring seats, were paddled across the smooth waters of Dal Lake to the houseboat. Rahim, our quiet houseboatman, introduced himself; and his father owned three houseboats, two on Dal Lake and one on the adjoining Nagir Lake, which was at that time occupied by three British ladies from the United Nations.

We reached the houseboat to be met by a smiling man who was Rahim's father. The two houseboats which lay alongside each other were both delightfully furnished and much more comfortable than anything we had expected. We found it very hard to find fault with either.

We went onto the top deck of the one we thought the better. The chairs were a little ramshackle and not enough for our number so more were brought. We settled down and began to talk business. "You can stay here and have all your meals for only seven-and-a-half rupees per person per day," said Rahim. Now we thought that there really must be a catch since this was the first offer and well below the government price of thirty rupees. "I will also," he continued, "come in your car and show you everything in Kashmir."

"Our car is already full – there is no room," we countered.

"You can bring everything here and then there will be room."

We still thought there must be a catch. "Does the houseboat leak?" we asked.

"No, Sir."

"Will you give us one rupee for every drop of water that enters the boat?"

"Yes, Sir, I will do that," replied Rahim, smiling.

Everything seemed to be in order so we made our final offer: "Can you promise us two days of undiluted happiness for twenty rupees per day for the three of us?"

"Yes, Sir," said Rahim and began at once to arrange

a seven day schedule for us, despite our request for two.

We returned to the shore, picked up our baggage, put the car away in some grounds belonging to a friend of Rahim, and returned to the houseboat. One hundred eyes were upon us. They were those of a legion of merchants and traders who constantly paddle about the lakes looking for the chance to trade. All sorts came out in the shikaras to see us: barbers, cashmere wool sellers, tailors, carpet makers, dealers in Kashmir arts and crafts, fruit sellers, grocers – the works. Insist as we might that we did not want to buy anything, they would say, "Let me show you ..." and their wares would be laid out on the deck. To say that you liked the look of something was tantamount to a firm order unless you were very careful.

One of their number stood out from all the rest, as he brought no wares and nor did he seem to force anything upon us, but he was an oriental merchant par excellence. This was Mr Meer, a dealer in Kashmiri arts and crafts, who seemed to have decided that he would have our trade to the exclusion of all other merchants in Srinagar. He told us of the great orders he had fulfilled for US department stores, of how he was at present fulfilling an order of 10,000 rupees for Liberty of London. He said that he would send his shikara the very next morning to take us into Srinagar to visit his showrooms. He made himself quite at home and sat on the deck looking across the water long after he had finished talking to us.

The dinner prepared for us that night by Rahim's cook was good, and we all thought that we had chosen well and might well spend longer in Kashmir than the two days we had planned.

Mr Meer was prompt. He had said that he would arrive at nine o'clock but when we entered the living room for breakfast at half past eight he was waiting for

us. Lying off was his three man-powered shikara. We had
breakfast, stepped aboard, reclined on the seats under
the awnings amidships and the three paddlers swung into
piston-like action. Across the smooth water patched with
lilies, loti and weeds we sped, past the houseboats that
lined the lakeside, past slower but more business-like and
austere shikaras than our own, into the narrow channel
that leads from the lake to the centre of Srinagar. This
was lined with houseboats too but of a different nature.
These looked more like floating barns with thatched
roofs, aboard which dwelt many of the inhabitants of
Srinagar whose whole life pivoted on the water. We saw
the women washing in it and the children playing and
splashing about in it.

We landed at a hard camber some way from Mr
Meer's showrooms. These were two rooms full of
sculpted furniture, ornate tables carved in a hundred
designs, lamp standards cut out in the form of Chinese
dragons and engraved jewel cases. He farmed the labour
out to families in the surrounding villages; some was so
precise and exacting that they could only work for two
or three hours each day.

Our time in Kashmir was idyllic: days spent out in
the hills with Rahim as our guide, leaving the car in a
village and hiring bony old ponies to take us further
into the hills. Rahim's picnic lunches, or tiffins, were a
delight. From his large basket he would produce cold
cutlets, potatoes and fruit. Then, to make tea, he had
a little portable samovar which burned charcoal to boil
the water. We went to Pahalgam to visit the source of the
Jhelum, one of the great tributaries of the Indus. It arose
from seven springs from the mountain at Kohanag and
produced a huge amount of water.

One day, Mr Meer, who employed a Persian cook,

invited us to a Persian lunch. This was wonderful news for us as we had been missing something of the gastronomic pleasures of Persia while we had been there. The meal consisted of over twenty-five courses, one after the other in very rapid succession. Sometimes we had not finished the dish we were eating when the next one appeared. The food was extremely good; spicy but the spice was not as hot as in India. The basis of the meal was three sorts of rice upon which was placed a wide variety of prepared meat and vegetable dishes. We ate the meal off the floor, sitting cross-legged on the carpet. Mr Meer also sat with us, but as a Persian host, was prevented by etiquette from eating with us. It was his duty to see that we were properly served and waited upon. This required that at no time were our plates to be empty.

When we had finished and he had satisfied himself that we were replete, he said, "Now, perhaps you will permit me to go and eat my meal?" He went out to be replaced by his brother who suggested a siesta. Feeling rather full, we agreed and he rolled out a large and very beautiful pile carpet. We took a cushion as our pillow and laid ourselves out for half an hour.

We talked to Mr Meer about trade in the Orient. We were given the impression that here was one part of the world where, as far as trade was concerned at any rate, nationalism counted for little. The very localisation of the manufacture and sale of the various commodities made the market an international one. This is not to say that trade and manufacture in the East is entirely stabilised and the manufacture and sale of wares cannot move from their traditional centres – for example, much of the market for Persian type carpets has moved from Kerman and other Persian cities to Pakistan. The advent of the American tourist has resulted in many Persian merchants taking undue advantage of the foreigner and raising prices to an unrealistic level. The Pakistanis have spotted this and undercut the Persian prices considerably.

Rahim had tears in his eyes when we left after five days of the "undiluted happiness" he had promised us. We were rather sad ourselves but we had to go, for we only had a little more than three weeks before we had to be in Ceylon. We drove back over the hills and down the same road we had ascended. It was on this journey that toilet paper came to our rescue. The steel bands that gripped the leaves of the left hand rear spring gave up the effort of holding the spring together on the multitudinous hairpin bends that led us over the pass. Admittedly, in our effort to make up time we had approached them with some vigour. Anyhow, there was a big clunk as we came out of a particularly severe hairpin and they had gone. We got out to see what we could about this latest mishap. The wire we used to bind them together did not seem as though it was going to stand the strain. A man in an old Chevrolet truck stopped to see what he could do to help us. We had a bracket which was too large for the binding job but our helper used two fresh toilet rolls to pack the job. This seemed to hold and our Heath Robinson arrangement was to last us until a garage in Delhi some 400 miles on.

We never received the goods we had ordered and paid for from Mr Meer. They must have been lost in transit. He had shown us a side of Kashmir life that we might never had seen. Furthermore, few of his goods would have fitted in the English decorative context. He had been a pleasure to deal with, though, and I am pleased that we met and traded with him. I had spent £40 with him.

That night we stayed in the rest house in Pathankot, 300 miles from Delhi, which we covered the next day. Once back on the "Grand Trunk Road", as routes joining the main Indian cities are called, we could make more speed. The roads were better and slightly wider, but the sacred cows and water buffaloes, although perhaps something of a joke in England, were a real menace. They would be grazing on the roadside, then quite suddenly, usually just as the car was approaching, wander out into the middle of the road. Humans, too, seemed just as capricious.

Cars were rare in India. We calculated that Indian rural pedestrians needed two blasts of the horn. The first was to tell, or at any rate remind, them that there were such things as motor cars and that they travelled faster than cows or donkeys, and the second blast was to warn them that this motor car was indeed coming towards them and would they please get off the road or at least leave us enough room to get past.

Naturally, if we were, as frequently happened, to come across the two obstacles at the same time – that is to say, a herd of cattle being led or driven along the road by farmers – further complications arose. The herdsmen were reluctant to do anything about their obstructing animals, even when we were right behind them. We solved this by obtaining a rod with which to poke the cattle which came within reach of the front passenger seat. We usually succeeded in moving them then.

Whenever we used this rod the farmers, far from being annoyed, were amused. It was not very long before we began to laugh at it all ourselves. A lesson we learned was that tourists won't change the habits or tempo of a country and they will enjoy themselves far more if they don't try. The strangest experience we had with a sacred cow was when we queued behind one to buy stamps in the Lucknow Post Office.

VI

Meeting Mr Nehru

We slept a comfortable night in our camp beds in the dak bungalow at Pathankot.

By teatime the following day, we had travelled the remaining descent from the foothills of the Himalayas into Delhi. We passed through Jullundur (Jalandhar) where many British postal workers are alleged to spend their retirements, living the high life on their pensions and a lower cost of living. We passed Ambala where the road comes in from Shimla to the north-east.

We could reflect on the most extraordinary adventure we had so far enjoyed. Delhi would be the climax of our expedition. We had completed in excess of 8,000 miles. Although we didn't know it, this was almost the halfway point of our driving.

We had traversed Europe, Turkey and Iran, taking a detour to the Caspian Sea and visiting Persepolis. We had travelled into Pakistan, across the Baluchistan Desert, turning north to Afghanistan through Kandahar and Kabul, making a detour to Bamiyan to see the giant Buddhas hewn out of the rock face, and Band-i-Amir to swim in its weird natural lakes. Returning to Pakistan by the Khyber Pass, we had crossed to India, then turned left to reach Kashmir.

To be fair, our Austin A40, with many repairs, had

withstood all this; however, its rear suspension was propped up with two toilet rolls as we rolled into Delhi. At 4 o'clock, the British High Commission was still open. Our embassies and high commissions accepted and held mail for us throughout the trip. They were always obliging and friendly. We called first at the Residency where we were directed to the office, an attractive modern building.

John already had a fixed date of return agreed with his future employer. He was to fly from Johannesburg on 13 October and had a ticket to do so. Now, both Robin and I received letters that put a check on our travels. I received a letter from my elder brother, John, inviting me to join our Newcastle department store on 8 November to run the Christmas decorations department. I accepted. It was to be the beginning of a sometimes fiery relationship between three brothers, but which would lead to a family department store business becoming a national store group.

Robin had a telegram of more immediate import. He had to return for an exam in five weeks' time. We all knew at once that this meant he would not be able to go to Africa. John and I found it hard to believe. In seven weeks of travel, thrills and excitement, we had become one. Two things prevented us from thinking that we should all finish in Colombo. First, it was the Cambridge Indo–African Expedition. This was inscribed on the car back and front. We felt obliged to do what it said on the tin. Second, Robin would not hear of such a plan and insisted we went on. We were deeply disappointed to be losing him – for his company, yes, but also for his expertise and strength of character.

Our gloom was increased by having no further news of a ship from Colombo to Aden. Even the Delhi beggar boys seemed less friendly than elsewhere. We rewarded the first one who gave us a smile with greater generosity. Our morale rose further when, booking in at the YMCA, we turned round to meet the welcoming smiles of the five members of the Cambridge Kashmir Expedition. We dined together, us telling them of the Dal Lake and Pahalgam and them telling us how to arrange to meet Prime Minister Nehru, which they planned to do the next morning.

With that, they stepped into their aged Land Rover, which could muster no more than 45 mph, and vanished into the black Delhi night, heading for the Hindu temple where they had found beds. There were some strange people on the Indian road.

For us, Delhi continued to be dull the following day. We needed contacts and we had none apart from the chance of meeting Mr Nehru. We motored about looking for a garage that would repair our car. The Austin agent we found had not heard of us and showed little interest. We were told of a Herr Kunze, the Mercedes agent, but could not find his workshop. At five o'clock we came across the British Motor Company where Mr O'Brien from County Cork said he would deal with the car the next day. This allowed us to do some sightseeing, primarily the Red Fort which enclosed a whole series of beautiful palaces that had been a last British holdout during the Indian mutiny of 1857. Although Government House was closed for the day, the government offices were not. We found the one that would grant us permission to meet the prime minister and arranged this for the next morning.

A Vespa powered tricycle taxi took us there the following day. Nehru had a dainty house that had been built for Lord Kitchener when he was commander-in-chief of the Indian Army. It had a mature garden that seemed almost overgrown. The prime minister was plainly not a man who stood on too much ceremony.

We were shown into a moderate sized anteroom almost divided in half by a large grand piano, the top of which was crowded with silver framed portraits, mainly of leaders who were either seeking or had sought freedom from their colonial masters. These included General Nasser, whose city of Port Said I had invaded as a member of the British Armed Forces in an effort to prevent his nationalisation of the Suez Canal, Archbishop Makarios who had inspired the EOKA revolt to drive the British out of Cyprus, the future President Kenyatta of Kenya who had organised the Mau Mau Rebellion, and President Sukarno who had driven out the Dutch from Indonesia; in short, these people were Britain's opponents. There could be no more poignant demonstration of our host's influence on the successful founding of the post-colonial era. He was its veritable father – the same man who had worked with Louis Mountbatten and others to secure the independence of India in 1947 and its subsequent partition from Pakistan. It was logical but nonetheless surprising for us, to be suddenly brought aware of his position on the world stage.

But this was only one aspect of his influence and power. At that time, China was a much more dormant force, so the indigenous powers in South and Southeast Asia all looked to Nehru for guidance. He had the respect of Soviet Russia to which India exported great quantities of textiles and other goods. This is to say nothing of his enormous power over India itself which had a population of 450 million then but which has since trebled, despite efforts to contain it.

In some ways, Asia is the new "New World", and at its centre is Delhi. A visitor from the West can be startled by the simple fact that in Delhi, Moscow stands to the west, not east, and the country stands protected from the "Great Bear" by the buffer states of Pakistan, Afghanistan and Iran. That morning Nehru had interior problems to deal with in the Kashmir and Naga areas. Sometimes other regions and peoples would cause him and his successors problems, but with the Himalayas between India and China, and the sea on two sides of its cartographical triangle, India has a strong geographical strategic position.

Opposite the grand piano in the anteroom was an unopened French window that held back the burgeoning garden that would have burst in upon the carpet had it been unlatched. We were positioned by the entrance door facing the wall, down which there was a narrow staircase with a solid balustrade. In front of the staircase stood a South African couple with their guide. In front of the French window stood a German pair who were in India to help build a steel mill. There were eight of us. Who was this modest man of such power and influence who bothered to see the likes of us on a regular basis?

We had been asked for at half past eight. Nehru slowly descended the stair about twenty minutes later followed, to our pleasure, by his daughter, Indira Gandhi, who was one day to succeed him. They both talked to everyone, coming to us last. Nehru had studied at Trinity College Cambridge, so he wanted to talk to us about the university, but he soon had to move on. But this was not before he had given us a real impression of his natural patience.

Indira Gandhi lingered. She also wanted to talk to us about Cambridge. She told us that she was wondering whether to send her son, Rajiv, there or to Munich University. We said what we could to help her. Thus, it was that morning we talked with both the present and the next prime minister and discussed the education of a third.

We pondered this experience over a milkshake in Wengers, the fashionable milk bar in Connaught Circus nearby. We then walked up the magnificent Rajpath towards Government House, flanked at the Rajpath's end by government legislative and administrative buildings. This was the superb concept of the two British architects, Baker and Lutyens. It was a fine conclusion to the outward signs of British imperial rule.

In the evening we had dinner in Delhi's top restaurant of the time – the Volga in Connaught Place, which specialised in Russian dishes. We had the speciality, "Bomb Volga". This was a souped-up version of Chicken Kiev. Wine was denied us due to the prohibition of alcohol. We missed its digestive aid and suffered the lack of it for the next twenty-four hours. Notwithstanding this, Bomb Volga remained a fond memory for us of Delhi.

There are many Indias, and we were off to see some more. We had once again had the car's suspension overhauled and we hoped that it would last us for a longer stretch this time. The radio too, a sponsorship gift from Smith's Industries, had been overhauled and was in fine fettle.

Moreover we were off to Jaipur, a city of Aladdin if ever there was one. As Mr Meer had told us in Srinagar, it was famed for its jewels, silk, and fine palaces. Having left Delhi in the afternoon, darkness was falling as we reached our targeted rest house outside the village of Shapura, about 100 miles from Jaipur. Our spirits had recovered; we had had a good, even exciting, certainly memorable stop in New Delhi. The new radio was working again and the countryside was more varied. There was plenty for us to be cheerful about. That evening its green hills were crowned by a beautiful Indian sunset. It was true that twice we came across monsoon floods that covered the road but these were just a warning of what was to come, and no real obstacle at this time. We had to be careful, however, as our car had the old-fashioned distributor delivering its sparks to the combustion chambers and we did not want them to become damp and inoperable. August was, after all, the monsoon's time.

Once ensconced in the rest house, we discovered that we had no rice or fruit, so I walked off into the village to buy some. It was not long before I had a crowd around me watching my choice of pears and runner beans and listening to me haggling over the price. When at last I had bought everything we required, a boy who had been carrying the purchases in his apron found a barrow made of planks and two bicycle wheels and laid everything on that. The crowd insisted on my sitting on the barrow and being wheeled back to the rest house while they followed on. Thus, we soon had an audience for our cooking too.

We arrived in Jaipur in time for lunch, but during the morning we had stopped in Amber. This was the old city of Jaipur, created by rulers of the ninth century. They had erected a palace, Italian style, right up on a hill. Much of it had been decorated at that time too. It was an emphatic forerunner of Florentine Renaissance work, and made it plain to us that oriental art, by means of the tales, sketches, and souvenirs of travellers, had been the foundation of Renaissance work in western Europe. What we need to remember when considering this time lapse in artistic influence is distance, the greater expense when western Europe was subject to the ravages of nearby states and the natural conservatism which is ever the problem of princely power. We have the likes of the Sforzas of Milan and the Medicis of Florence and their contemporary Italian potentates much to thank for this fantastic artistic revolution in the middle of the millennium, which naturally took centuries to work through from traveller's tales to sponsors' or princes' patronage. The ideas were wonderful but needed money and a more secure state to ensure their progress.

In Amber it was the carving and paintwork that suggested the Italian Renaissance so much to it. Throughout the Middle East and India other artistic media could be seen leading the way for the western Renaissance.

Driving in India was often fairly fast (say 50 mph), the surfaces of the roads were good and monsoon floods were infrequent. Sacred cows paid no attention to motor cars and there seemed to be as many cows as humans. Animal life became more colourful. We frequently passed peacocks (also sacred) and saw our first two elephants (sacred too). Monkeys lived in the roadside trees.

We spent the afternoon in Jaipur. It was a busy town: many beggars, many shops with much noise and babble. We visited one or two jewel shops. We made it plain before going in that we were not there to buy, but the owners were pleased and proud to see us.

After touring the walls of Jaipur, we found the way out of town. The exits and entrances to Indian towns are often confusing. To assume that the main road into a town will lead you down the main street, might be misguided. Sometimes there is no main street, or if there is one, it may be blocked with cattle, donkeys, or haggling traders. So one's path with a motorcar must be chosen with caution.

On the road to Agra, the monsoon really hit us. Great sheets of rain flooded the fields, and often the road, as we drove. It continued for hours on end as an Indian monsoon rainstorm will. We came across one poor party from Agra in a Land Rover whose sump had holed and they had run out of oil. It was a pleasure to give them some. We surely had a debt to repay to the society of the road after all the favours we had received.

Our destination was the Dak Bungalow at Bharatpur, just thirty-six miles short of Agra, which we aimed to reach the following morning. Small wonder that the monsoon was at its worst as we approached it. We learned later that it is the centre of a broad depression, collecting rivers from the Himalayas which have formed marshes around the town. It is a magnificent bird sanctuary but a strong centre of the monsoon. What an exciting country!

As we searched for the Dak Bungalow, we kept passing a small but opulent palace. It could not possibly be that, we thought, it seemed far too grand. But it was. The former hunting lodge of the local maharajah had been given by him in forfeit to the state. We went into its luxurious shelter of chandeliers, white linen covered ottomans, beautiful carpets and luxury bedrooms. It was already occupied by a wealthy lawyer, Mr Gupta, his richest client, the portly Mr Tawari, and his svelte daughter; and Mr Gupta's astrologer, an essential attendant of any proper Indian advocate. "If the sun and moon affect our habits and doings, why should not the planets also?" he asked of us. There was no possible reply. We soon became friends.

They had been dealing with an exciting case of murder in the town. We got on well. Discovering that John was a Scotsman, they produced a flask of whisky which soon had us forget the rain. They invited us to visit them in Agra where they lived. They cursed the cooperative system that Nehru had forced upon them; they would prefer private arrangements rather than government systems so often riddled with graft and corruption. The Indian middle class established by Macaulay's influence, they were pleased to admit, was very individualistic.

The rain had stopped by morning. Before Agra we arrived at the abandoned city of Fatehpur Sikri. This was founded in 1569 by the emperor Akbar as a thanks offering for the birth of his son, Selim, and was to be the new capital of the Mughal Empire. However, the water there proved to be bad and less than fifty years after its foundation it was abandoned. Much of it still remains, including its surrounding wall which has a seven mile long circumference. Inside there are many beautiful buildings and a handsome mosque. A guide caught hold of us as soon as we arrived. Guides are a mixed blessing in India. Their information may be unreliable and they try to involve you with various expensive schemes. There were opportunities for such enterprise in mosques where you were often inveigled into the sanctuary of a priest who would show relics of the holy prophet and then demand a price and an order.

On to Agra, where we went directly to the Taj Mahal. When we saw it in 1960, the Taj Mahal had already become a cliché of sightseeing tourism. Particularly with the cynicism of youth, we expected to be a little disappointed with it, but not at all. For us the two most significant buildings that we encountered throughout the course of the expedition were Persepolis and the Taj Mahal.

Persepolis for its sheer size and strength. Yet it combined total balance with its dual purpose of a strategic fortress and a complete seat of power. This seat had overwhelming artistic support of that power, which has to make it the veritable apotheosis of a palace.

The Taj Mahal, however, has but a single utility, that of a mausoleum for a beloved woman. It has none of the mixed purpose and design expressed by Persepolis. In fact, it uses a very limited palette of cupola and white marble inlaid with black marble in classic Persian design. This has the effect of enhancing the white with a greater force of brightness brought about by the contrast. Then the pools that both lead to, and reflect, the building in a broken but balanced pattern add a vital tranquility and thoughtfulness. Indeed, if you will, it also brings a sense of condolence.

Dawn is the best time to visit, as Robin demonstrated. Later, a few people will arrive to wash their hands and face in the pool. This is no sacrilege, simply Indian acceptance and use of what is available to them and thus being part of the scene that so much links the wider community with India's sudden expressions of wealth. This is rather the same effect as with the golden temple of the Sikhs in Amritsar.

Persepolis and the Taj Mahal have these clear elements in common: purpose and balance. Beauty, as ever, is truth.

With the sky full of monsoon clouds, the white marble against the black inlay appeared dazzling. Driving out of the gate as we left we found the way blocked by twelve-year-olds with kukris to sell, and ranged behind them were more mature salesmen whose line was snake-charming.

We had not met with snake-charmers before but we had been warned of their wiles. We stopped when John, who was sitting in front, had a kukri thrown into his lap with "Ten rupees" barked in his left ear. Quick as a flash, Robin, who was driving, slipped into gear and we began to move off with the kukri. This produced cries of anger which didn't stop until we halted again. More kukris were pushed into the car, but before long the boys were shoved aside by their senior colleagues, the snake-charmers. One of these thrust the face of a rather bilious looking snake through the window, while another held a mongoose in his arms, offering to show us a fight between the two for three rupees. Another man, sitting in the background with his basket, began to charm a snake. It appeared out the basket, steadied its head, and bit the charmer. The climax came when another hawker tried to sell us a set of charming pipes and was somewhat taken aback when John produced his bagpipe chanter and played that to them. We bought a kukri from the boys, some peacock feather fans from the men and parted on good terms.

That day, we could not contact our friends at the guesthouse. In the afternoon, we visited the Taj Mahal again. Set on the banks of the Jumna, which flows down from Delhi, It is situated two miles from the city centre and approached through a large park. Its surroundings are rather scruffy, but as with the Blue Mosque in Istanbul, the eye is so riveted with the beauty and the supreme distinction of the building itself, that its surroundings are immaterial. To me, the most striking feature I found is the contrast brought about by the inlay work of the black marble within the white.

It has been said that the Taj Mahal is now falling into decay, and the preservation schemes set in motion by Lord Curzon have not been maintained. However, there was very little outward evidence of this and we found nothing to detract from the wonder of the spectacle. There is tremendous anticipation engendered when approaching such a celebrated building, mingled with the fear of disappointment. Parking the car on arrival, ignoring the cries of prospective guides who rushed up the steps of the enormous archway that leads through to the mausoleum, there was no disappointment for us. It dazzles the eye from first to last with a paramount and lasting brilliance.

Later, we made friends with certain guides, some of whom were about our age. They envied us our enormous privileges but never coveted them. The Indian youths that we spoke to were full of curiosity about anything we could tell them, and if their questions were a little naïve, how much more so must have been our questions and thoughts about India.

Robin was up before all of us the next morning to photograph the Taj Mahal in the early sunlight when the long waters are entirely still, like a mirror. By the time John and I joined him, a guide was making his ablutions in one of the pools. After breakfast we went round to the city offices of our friend, Mr Gupta. It was Indian Independence Day, and large crowds mingled in the street waiting to see a large band march past pursued by children. We found Mr Gupta sitting in his office in the company of Mr Tewari (or Fatty as he had come to be called) and a tax collector. We chatted with them for some time and then Mr Gupta invited us to Independence Day lunch. Wealth, in India, is something to be enjoyed and its pleasure shared.

Lunch was with the Guptas in their house overlooking the lawn and Taj Mahal. Being Independence Day it had a festive flavour. Reminiscent of a description by Charles Dickens of Sunday lunch in a middle-class home, present were Mr Gupta and his wife, their two small children, Mr Tewari (Fatty did not sit at the table but on a couch behind) and Mr Tewari's eldest son. Great pains were taken to see that the children behaved themselves and made the minimum of noise. Mrs Gupta kept worrying about the food and looked at first embarrassed and then delighted when we asked her for the recipe for one of the dishes. She said it was a secret. When we were finished, the children were summoned to give us a recital. First, they sang a song in Urdu, then recited "Baa Baa Black Sheep" in English. I had never come across so much warmth and cordiality in such a short acquaintance. He told us that he was married at the age of six to a girl aged four. When talking to such an obviously civilised and cultured man, we were much less inclined to cast off such practices as outlandish; such customs could well lead to a more stable society, which in many ways it was.

After lunch, we spent the worst night of the entire trip at a rest house 150 miles along the road to Cawnpore (now Kanpur). The air was hot and heavy, the rice we cooked went all wrong, we couldn't sleep for the noise of Independence celebrations which went on till dawn. We funked breakfast in the morning and were on the road to Cawnpore before seven, heading through that city for Lucknow – the centre of the Indian Mutiny.

We visited the ruined residency where, for ninety-nine days between August and November 1857, a dwindling British force held out against the mutineers. As we toured the site of the siege, we wondered at the fortitude of the besieged. The residency and its outbuildings occupy perhaps the most strategic spot in the town. It has its back to the river, but the hill upon which the building stood is raised only a little above the surrounding area. I cannot imagine how they were able to defend the position for so long against superior odds and racked by disease. At some bastions, apparently, the attackers were at such close quarters that they would exchange jibes. We had felt the same when we studied the Red Fort in Delhi, which had suffered in similar circumstances but held out. Perhaps as with other Anglo–Indian relationships, disagreements were never totally hostile.

We were over halfway through August now and there was much motoring to be done if we were to reach Colombo by the end of the month. We held council and decided to head for the holy city of Benares (Varanasi) that afternoon and make that the easternmost point in our itinerary. After that, we would head for Bombay to pursue a zigzag path down India by going on from there to Madras (Chennai), Bangalore (Bengaluru), Madurai and Mandapam, then the ferry to Ceylon (Sri Lanka).

As for time, we had planned a four-month trip and had already expended two. Robin was to leave us in two weeks' time and only half of our motoring was done. Besides the need for regular repairs to the car, we had to cross the Indian Ocean to Aden without, at this point, knowledge of a ship that would take us. Then we had to find passage to Eritrea, again, without knowledge of any ship. The Johannesburg wedding date was 8 October. We were certainly right to decide to turn west and south at Benares, foregoing our eastern ambition of Calcutta. We had to make up time, and more obstacles were to come.

We therefore drove back down the fast road to Cawnpore and over the Ganges again to rejoin the Grand Trunk Road between Delhi and Calcutta, which follows that most sacred of rivers as far as Benares. The road crosses the river again at Allahabad, which is where it is joined by the River Jumna whose water has already flowed past Delhi and Agra. The Ganges and Jumna are both "most holy rivers" and the place where they meet is called Sangum, a most holy place. These "holy" locations are of vital importance in Indian society. Arriving there at nightfall, we searched for a rest house, but finding none we had dinner in a local cafe and pressed on for an hour out of town before we began to look for a camping spot. Often, when we thought we had found a good clear bit of field, it would turn out to be a paddy field so we would motor on. At last we found a suitable place and settled down to a good rest in our first night camping since Afghanistan.

In the morning we only had a few miles drive into Benares. We had heard much against Benares – that it was smelly and dirty. Being a city that attracts not only Western tourists but also vast numbers of Hindu pilgrims from all over India, it has naturally drawn a large number of profiteers, wide boys and generally unsavoury characters anxious to take advantage of innocent strangers wherever they may come from. When we first arrived, we looked for the Monkey Temple and arrived at the gates of the Hindu University. I went in to ask the porter in the lodge where we might find the Monkey Temple. He gave us long directions which took us through the grounds of the university, and he even gave us a ticket authorising us to pass through the grounds. Off we drove, but at last had to return, having had a good tour of the university but never seeing anything that might remotely resemble the Monkey Temple. I explained to the porter that I must have misunderstood his directions as we had seen no sign of the temple.

"Ah, no," he laughed, "but was not the university beautiful?" It had, in fact, been impressive. "I wanted you to see it," he said. Then he gave us totally different directions to the temple which took us in the opposite direction.

We soon found ourselves attracted to the water's edge. Here we met Kasimat, a boatman. He was a personality. He had a loincloth around his middle and he had the blackest and shiniest body that we had ever seen. He was like a big elm tree, two gnarled feet growing into two thick muscular legs and a big pot belly bulging over his loincloth. That was Kasimat from the ground up! Most striking was his face: two benevolent dark eyes, fiery enough to set the Ganges on fire, gazed over a large moustache and wide, generous mouth.

"I am Kasimat," he announced. "I will take you on the river for three rupees." We tried to haggle but he was immovable. There was no arguing with Kasimat.

VII

Monsoon

Allowing for local exaggeration, the Ganges was fifty feet above its normal level at this time; another eight feet higher, we learned, and parts of Benares would be flooded, as indeed happened shortly after we left. Despite its depth, the river flowed past in great yellow eddies. So deep were the waters that the Smallpox Temple was entirely inundated and only a ragged pennant protruded marking its location. Kasimat's boatmen did not look half as strong as he was. But having come so far, we had to go on the river so we stepped aboard.

The boatmen's ploy was to drag the craft upstream using the part-flooded buildings at the side of the river and, where they could not do this, they would combat the immensely strong current with their oar-like paddles. All went well for the first fifty yards but then we hit difficulties. We had been pulled to the end of one of the temples which jutted out from a ghat, one of those broad sets of steps leading down to the water where the pilgrims would come to immerse themselves. Water rushed around the corner of the building. The boatmen were not trying very hard to continue our upstream course. They could not be persuaded to progress until another boat carrying a fellow tourist casually overtook us, and the boatmen were shamed into greater efforts, bringing us our three rupees worth.

"Jumna, Ganges, most holy rivers, most holy rivers," pronounced the Brahmin priest with emphasis. He had invited himself to join our party. We had already refused his services as a guide when we had met him before but he had squeezed into the boat and, once in midstream, Kasimat blackmailed us to let him guide us around the temples on our return. "Look, the burning ghats!" exclaimed the Brahmin. "Hindus burning their bodies, most holy." And on the bankside there was smoke rising from the funeral pyres of Hindus who believe that by this means they will have a better afterlife. It is said that since there is a fee charged for the use of the ghats in this way, the poorer people do not burn their bodies entirely but throw them into the river half charred. Thankfully we saw none float by.

To return downstream, the craft was steered into the middle of the river before allowing the current to carry it down. It was with some relief that we stepped ashore and allowed our Brahmin guide to lead us towards the Nepalese temple.

Away from the waterside, we went through the vegetable market, squeezed through narrow streets teeming with pilgrims, pickpockets and tradesmen, past temples, one against the other, each one groaning with incantations and prayers, past the temple of our Brahmin companion which he showed us with pride, and around yet another corner before we reached the Nepalese temple. "Many carvings, most obscene, look!" he exclaimed with glee, longing to see our reaction. Sure enough, the temple was covered with pornographic woodcarvings – beautifully done, of course. The atmosphere was vibrant and excitable.

We had stopped for bananas (at an anna each we lived off them), when the Allahabad chief of road services

Northwest Frontier

Mountain fort hewn out of the precipice.

A cold swim in the Band-e-Amir natural reservoir.

It is a hard life as a shepherd in Afghanistan.

Huge Buddha figure, at Bamyan, carved into the rock. Its face was removed in the 6th century; the whole was dynamited out of the rock by the Taliban since our visit.

Waterfall at Band-e-Amir.

Tea (or chai) at Band-e-Amir.

A bucolic Khyber Pass.

The Kohat Rifle Factory

Chris, trained and well used to handling the British service Lee Enfield Mark IV rifle, was astonished at the equal quality of the facsimiles produced without powered tools at the factory in the Kohat tribal area in Pakistan. The metal work was fine. The bolt action inserting the round into the chamber was smooth as silk.

Chris inspects a facsimile of the former British Lee Enfield service rifle.

Inspecting the inside works.

Simple technology.

Kashmir Houseboat Holiday

Shakira to Mr Meer's (on the left) factory.

One of his carpets.

Tiffin at Pahalgam where rises the Jhelum, grand tributary of the Indus.

John and Robin with Rahim in the Srinagar gardens.

Our houseboat.

Rahim, our houseboatman.

The Rajpath, New Delhi, with Government House at its end.

With Ali Tobraki in Tabriz.

Animals

Sacred cow.

Performing bear in
Turkish town.

Elephant in Amber.

Rivers

Kasimat, our Ganges boatman.

Gentle Jhelum.

Flooded Jumna.

Disappearing temple.

Bathing in the Ganges at Benares.

drew up alongside us to chat about our trip and offer us some advice: "You must turn south at Allahabad and go to Rewa. There you will see the only white lion in the world with black stripes – it is owned by the maharajah."

"You mean a zebra?" we asked, startled at hearing of this strange beast.

"No, it is a lion," he contradicted. "The only one like it in the world."

We have yet to solve the mystery of the black-striped white lion for we never arrived in Rewa. We were delayed by the first of the rivers that we had to cross, the Tons River. Twenty miles south of Allahabad we came to a village with a warning sign that we would come to dread in the following three days: a long line of trucks leading to the edge of a monsoon-swollen river. We drove past them to find our headlights reflecting a wide stretch of water, as the usual crowd of locals collected to watch how we would react to our predicament. We spoke to one poor motorist who had been waiting all day for the river to subside; he had taken French leave from his firm for a jolly time in Allahabad and now found himself stranded on the wrong side of the river, unable to return to his job. "What I can do?" as they say. Different expressions, same solution the world over: he had some rum, we had some whisky, and by midnight we seemed to have most of our problems solved.

We spent the night in Allahabad, and set off on a different route the next day. After four more hours at the wheel we hit the flooded Jumna River upstream from where it joins with the Ganges. In normal times a pontoon bridge was rigged across it, but this was dismantled during the monsoon season. Instead, one of the pontoons was used as a ferry and there was an old river tug in service to pull it across. Service was slow.

A railway bridge stared temptingly down on us from downstream, but although this was sometimes open to motor traffic to hobble across, it was not to be opened until late in the afternoon for this purpose. The local chief took us in hand; as we sat, cross-legged, over a cup of tea, he arranged that we would be last on – therefore first off – the pontoon ferry, except for the ubiquitous cows which were taken everywhere in India. While we waited I found an itinerant barber who gave me a good haircut. The chief, who had been most interested in our travels, spent the time passing on our story to any new arrivals to the scene.

The next day followed the same routine: a good start of four hours and then, "Oh, no," another long line of lorries leading down to the waterside of another river. This one was crossed by a causeway which was under three feet of water when we arrived. But rivers rise and fall very quickly in the monsoons, rarely being in flood for more than three days and often not more than twenty-four hours. This one was no exception. By the time we had mended a shackle, had some lunch, watched a calf being born to a water buffalo and chatted to a few of the locals, many of the waiting trucks had already passed through. It was deemed safe to progress, despite the advice of the crowd who urged us to wait for another hour. With a barefooted Robin leading the way to check that the causeway was secure, we ventured across. This precipitated a hero's send-off from the crowd, who seemed to be full of caution in that part of the world. But it was four o'clock by now and we had driven less than 300 miles that day. We found a place to camp by the roadside. Hordes of small black beetles got everywhere – all over the tent, our food and us. Despite these trespassers, we all slept well.

By nightfall the next day, we had reached Indore

in Central India, but we had lost so much driving time that we resolved to press on overnight to Bombay when we had eaten. So it was that we drew up outside the Lantern Hotel for dinner and alongside a Land Rover that, judging by the place names written all over it, had pursued – in reverse – exactly the same course that we had planned for ourselves. Apparently it had been driven through Africa to Kenya and then crossed to Ceylon and Southern India. The owners were the charming Mr and Mrs Massey of East 76th Street, New York who had come up from Bombay that day, and were not only able to tell us of a flooded river on the road but also how to avoid it. Thus unhindered, save for a broken down truck in the middle of the road just outside of Indore, we negotiated the Satpura mountain range and made good progress overnight. We reached Bombay by the middle of the next day, 400 miles from Indore, and just avoided the Balaghat Range. Make no mistake, India is very mountainous. It is a tough place to live.

After we had pierced its twenty-mile deep urban sprawl, Bombay was a surprise to us. Situated on a peninsula, the city of five million people straggles out from its centre which is situated towards the port. The seafront, known as "the necklace" at night, was impressive by any standards and not at all what we were expecting, the bay being lined with smart white, five or six storey buildings containing offices, flats and hotels. The best hotel in town was the Taj Mahal. Some say that the architect's plans were not interpreted correctly and it was built the wrong way round. It is situated by the Gateway of India, a commemorative archway constructed in honour of the visit of King George V in 1911. This was an imperial triumph and helped to keep India loyal over two world wars.

There are many hotels along the seafront of Bombay, but we chose the Delamar, both for its moderate charge and decent room we were given. This overlooked the Indian Ocean and the rate, including bathroom and meals for us all was twenty-three rupees (£3). The next day was Sunday, so we motored to Juhu Beach for a bathe in the mild surf. This must have changed much since British days. The few bathers were outnumbered by the ice cream and water-coconut vendors and twice the number of beggar boys. The ice creams came on sticks as lollipops, and the beggars were so desperate that they licked the last stains of ice cream from the sticks as soon as they hit the sand.

We met an Indian textile merchant there who had driven out with his wife in a new Austin A90. Such large cars were almost impossible to obtain in India, at any rate by legal means. This one, he told us, had been arranged for him by ICI with whom he did much business. Not only for this reason did he hold a high opinion of ICI, but he also found them to be straight people to do business with. If there was a price reduction between his order and delivery to him, he would always receive a credit note, and he could not say this for other firms. It was good to have a superior report of British industry.

VIII

South India

It is 900 miles south-west across the Deccan plateau to Madras from Bombay, and we had to be there by Tuesday night, which meant an overnight drive on the Monday. Garage repairs and flooded rivers had lost us time. Setting off on Monday afternoon, we reached Poona (Pune) just before dusk, and had time to tour the racecourse and look inside the old polo club building while daylight still lasted. We dined on fried eggs and bread further down the road in a guest house owned by a family of the Parsi faith. These people had once owned a liquor store; prohibition had forced them to close.

We arrived in Bangalore in the middle of the next morning. After brunch in a snack bar we went to Dozey's Garage which was yet another of those run by an Englishman. The radiator had developed a leak and while it was being repaired he told us of the paradise it had been for him in the days of the British. He had come out with his father in 1923. In those days, he told us, two of the richest cavalry regiments always used to be stationed in Poona and there was a dance every night.

The pressure of time to complete our expedition was now acute. Constant breakdowns, particularly effecting the rear end suspension of the car, meant garage delays at every principal town en route, but we had no more trouble with flooded rivers. Robin and John had become expert mechanics and at one point changed a rear spring in an hour and forty minutes. Reaching Colombo in good time was critical: Robin had to return for his exam, while John and I had to find a ship for Aden. In Bombay there had been good news and bad. Our friend John Jackson had invited us to stay in Colombo in an air conditioned bungalow, but another letter from the travel company could not confirm an Aden passage. They must have known of liners that had already left Australia with such a schedule. Small wonder that Thomas Cook was later nationalised.

The fraught 2,000 mile drive from Delhi to Madras had taken twelve days with "tourist stops" at Jaipur, Agra, Lucknow, Allahabad, Benares, Cawnpore and Bombay. These conveniently coincided with garage stops. Although these and flooded rivers represented delays, they had also been a chance to meet the people of Pakistan and India. Not only did they generally speak English but they also appeared to have the same sense of humour. We developed a lifelong affection for them.

We undertook two overnight drives within four days, one to reach Bombay and the other Madras. Over mountainous terrain the roads were emptier, not only of people but of cars too. We operated a strict two hour shift driving system and this worked well. The 900 mile Bombay–Madras stage, excluding stops, was accomplished in excess of an average of 40 mph.

Robin and John had a friend from the Newbury area living in Madras whom we had contacted. When we phoned from Bangalore, Peter Siggers very kindly invited us to stay in his Madras bungalow, colourfully called "Otti Castle". It seemed we would have a warm welcome there.

Peter shared Otti Castle with three other English bachelors. When I mentioned that it was my birthday the next day and that we would like to hold a small party for them, he replied that the next day also happened to be the third anniversary of his arrival in India and he would like to hold a party for us. Within twenty-four hours, thirty people were mustered while the servants laid on an array of Chinese food. The talk was mainly of the impending rugger festival which was to be held that weekend up in the hills at Otti Kumund. It was said to be cooler up there, not that it seemed to make a great deal of difference: on the night we arrived it must have been at least 80 degrees Fahrenheit.

We could not at first find Peter as he was playing rugby. (In Colombo, with heat of equal intensity, we found John Jackson doing exactly the same thing.) Most of the guests were British, and while they might admit that society was narrow they countered this by their ability to enjoy themselves. They appreciated their servants, their clubs and, some of them, their big game hunting. "We are an *SS Chusan* romance," chanted one handsome couple, who met on the P&O liner that had brought them out and who married on arrival. Life for them was fast and eventful and they made the most of it. But it was plain that they inhabited an enclosed world.

We had to go. We left Madras late the next afternoon and had only an hour's driving in daylight before darkness fell. The roads were good, well surfaced and wide in Madras state and we made fine progress. Then, as night fell, we had two accidents, one minor and the other major. Robin ran over a pig and then, when I took over, I ran into a huge rock higher than the underside of the car. Dazzled by the headlights of a parked stationary bus, I failed to spot a large jagged rock thirty foot in front of me. In a second, I knew I had only three options: I could direct through the sump and ruin the engine, rake the wheel over it and turn the car over, or run it through the right-hand suspension. I chose the last. It was a large boulder twelve inches high and two feet across. "Crunch" went the rock as it tore into the right flank of our front suspension at 30 mph. We came to an abrupt halt which brought the bodywork down onto the front wheel, putting the steering out of action. We slewed across to the wrong side of the road and finished, without overturning, in a thorn bush. The passengers from the bus came out to help us but there was little they could do. The vehicle was immobilised. We could not even push it without lifting the body off the wheel.

The position appeared hopeless. It was half past eight in the evening and we were fifteen miles from Trichinopoly (Tiruchirappalli), the next major town. It was unlikely that we would be able to find a breakdown truck at this hour, and if we could, the next day was a public holiday and even the Public Works Department truck, if there happened to be one, would not be operating. On top of this, it seemed as if this had really imperilled our plans to arrive in good time to find ourselves a ship from Colombo. However, none of these difficulties deterred the succession of wonderful people we were to meet from that moment on who were prepared to go out of their way to help us. One after the other, they did so.

At that moment a bus drew up that was going to Trichinopoly. The driver and passengers came over to see what the trouble was and the one passenger who could speak English said it was possible to go now to Trichinopoly and hire a truck. I therefore left Robin and John with the car and boarded the bus. Before we reached the town the only English speaking passenger got off. He left me in the hands of the driver. Having arrived at the terminus, the first thing he did was to drive me to the railway station where he bought me a coffee from the vegetarian buffet. He refused every effort that I made to pay for it. For an hour and a half afterwards, the bus driver – with me as the only passenger – drove around the town in an effort to find a truck owner who would take me out to recover the car. Remarkably, he eventually found a driver with a truck who agreed to pick me up at the bus station at three o'clock the next morning. Meanwhile, I was to sleep in the bus station. He rolled out a length of coconut matting over the concrete floor. I laid down, shut my eyes and even slept. I never saw the bus driver again.

Sure enough at three o'clock precisely the driver arrived with his truck. I climbed in and we returned to the car. John and Robin had not been idle. They had raised the car and inspected, as best they could, the extent of the damage. With difficulty, by dint of lowering the truck into a ditch, we loaded the car onto the truck.

The truck driver told us of a garage that would be open, despite the public holiday, and we had the car there before it opened. Again, fortune was for us the progeny of misadventure, for the garage manager revealed himself to be not only warm-hearted and helpful, but also very efficient. One reason for this was that he had been on a course at the General Motors factory in Detroit, Michigan. Despite his kindness and efficiency, however, and his willingness to turn half his mechanics on to our car since we were tourists, it was evident that repairs were going to take at least two days. "Everything is a little out of line," he understated. For this reason, Robin took the train to Colombo to be sure of catching his plane and to enquire of a ship going to Aden. John and I checked into the Ashby Hotel and went to see *Rio Bravo* with John Wayne at the cinema. It was a great year for films. In Lahore, we had seen *It Started with a Kiss* with Glenn Ford and Debbie Reynolds.

The garage did not let us down, and within two days (one a public holiday, the other a Saturday) John and I were on the move once more. The price of the work was £30. That evening we reached the quarantine camp at Mandapam, a village at the southern tip of India where the road ends. It was necessary to put both car and ourselves aboard the train to travel further south over Adams Bridge to Dhanushkodi, the ferry port for Ceylon. Adams Bridge is a bridge only in name for the straits between India and Ceylon are as wide as the straits of Dover. The water between the two countries is shallow and few ocean-going ships can pass. Proposals to dredge undersea, greatly reducing the length of a round India maritime passage, have been resisted in the interests of trade for the ports of Colombo and Trincomalee.

Mandapam was desolate: the people were poor, agriculture was difficult and food hard to obtain. Even at the rest house we were told that we could have a bed for the night but no food could be provided. We were lucky enough to meet a helpful customs officer who, when he had supervised the loading of our car aboard the railway wagon that was to take it to Dhanushkodi pier, offered to have his wife make us some supper that he would bring over to us at the rest house. We did not deserve this good fortune.

He brought it over himself and, obviously glad to have the company of two new faces, stayed for a chat. He apologised for it being a vegetarian meal for not only was there a shortage of meat in the area, but he was also a strict Hindu – although not as strict as his father who had refused to eat a meal in his house because he believed that meat had once been eaten there. He went on to tell us of the hardships in India and in particular those of the Tamils in the extreme south. Sixty per cent of Indians, he told us, had never tasted milk save from their mother's breast. With the population increase, efforts to grow more food were often nullified since there are more mouths to feed. Certain people, not realising this fact, had even wished for the days of the British again.

We questioned him about his job. Apparently smuggling, chiefly gold or opium, was common. There was bribery on both sides of the law and an informant would often receive as much as fifty per cent of the value of the seized contraband made as a result of his disclosures. Cochin (Kochi) is a famous base for smuggling and the major port in south-west India. One day in that port, police and customs officials had definite information that a dhow in the harbour contained contraband gold. They searched it for three days but they had no success. At last the customs men held a desperate conference on board the dhow. In his exasperation, one of the officers scraped the side of the ship with his penknife. Little by little he revealed a gleam in the ship's side. It was gold: every nail and rivet that held the dhow together was made of gold.

We travelled by train and then by boat to Ceylon. Coming down the gangplank at Talaimannar, we met a man who was trying to squeeze his way up it. "Mr John?" he enquired to our surprise when he saw us. "Mr Chris?"

"Well, yes," we replied, uncertainly.

"Aah!" he exclaimed, delightedly, "Mr Rodriguez, a friend of Mr Robin, left a message that I was to meet you off the boat and look after you." This was teamwork indeed.

Robin had told us of Mr Rodriguez, someone he

had met on the train, when we had telephoned him in Colombo before we left Trichinopoly. It was great work by Robin, not to mention the kindness of the gentleman himself. He saw to it that we received the car safely off the ship, arranged for us to have dinner aboard the boat train while it lay at the quayside before leaving for Colombo, and – best of all – arranged that we should sleep in the customs officers' bungalow not far from the quayside. He also made sure that we were able to telephone Robin from the station master's office and then, leaving us in the hands of two customs officials, we parted. The next morning, having had coffee with the two officials, we took our leave of them. By late lunchtime (the rear shackle up to its old tricks again but as yet holding fast) we turned into the road where the Jacksons lived, and had kindly asked us to stay, to find Robin just setting out on a bathing expedition.

John Jackson was working for Shell in Ceylon, and since one of his colleagues who lived just down the road was away on leave, he had most happily arranged for us to stay at his house. Diana Jackson welcomed us before we went off to have a much needed bath. Little Jonathan Jackson, who was three commented, "Mummy, they must be very dirty – they are having a bath and a shower!"

While we showered and read our mail, Robin told us of his adventures since he had left us in Trichinopoly. He had changed for Mandapam and spent the night at its quarantine camp, then caught the train for Dhanushkodi and the Ceylon ferry. On the train he met Ignatius Rodriguez, a Ceylonese. He learned from him of the poor state of Ceylon's economy and how Mr Nehru had starved the south by taking two-thirds of their rice for the north.

Robin travelled overnight by train to Colombo,

finding rail travel in Ceylon more comfortable than in southern India. After breakfasting with Rodriguez, he rang the Jacksons and later met John and Diana Jackson and they went out to dinner with them.

Although we had been told there were no ships to Aden, when Robin targeted P&O that Monday in Colombo, he was offered four ships within the week that would take us there. When we mentioned wanting a passage to Ethiopia from Aden, George Gater, the efficient P&O representative there, could not understand where the difficulty lay. He merely sent a telegram to his colleague, Martin Watts, in Aden, to book us on their first ship leaving for Massawa after our arrival in Aden.

SS Strathnaver was sailing on the following Sunday and the *Canton* two days after that. Robin had also visited and lined up Walker Brothers, the Austin agents and the Norwich Union insurance agents preparatory to the arrival of the A40 in Colombo. He ends his diary entry that day with: "Just setting off for a swim after lunch when the A40 comes down the road."

We took our hosts out to dinner at the Little Hut, a restaurant in the Mount Lavinia Hotel. The last time I had sat at table with John was for a coffee some ten months before with his brother, Peter, in Fenwick's. Here, he told us stories of the romance of the Orient.

The Austin garage, which had had the car overnight, told us that it was in a worse state than we feared, despite the repairs in Trichinopoly. The chassis was twisted and certain essential joints had been structurally weakened. The manager, Mr Stables, told us that it would take two or three weeks to put it in perfect order again. We could not afford this time, so we asked him to do what he could by Sunday, our sailing date. It was Wednesday.

The cost of our passage was a rude shock to us for

the price we were quoted for two passengers and the car was £67, more than double the estimate given to us in England, with loading and unloading charges to be added at either end. There seemed to be no alternative to accepting the charges. By this time we had come so far, overcome so many small and nagging difficulties, that our purpose had gained a momentum which would need much to break it. Furthermore, in terms of effort, we had reached the point of no return: Africa lay between us and England so it was, in a sense, almost as easy to stop off and journey through Africa before returning home. The prices do not seem so high today!

We went to see Tom Bayne, the Norwich Union insurance agent. He was most kind and sympathetic towards us. It was well within his power, even his duty, to delay us for three weeks in Colombo while the car was completely and permanently repaired. He did not. He saw how urgent it was to us to be on our way as soon as possible, and so agreed that as long as reasonably efficient and firm repairs were made on the car – efficient and strong enough to carry us safely through Africa – he was prepared to let us go at the end of the week. Since that rock on the road to Trichinopoly, everyone had been miraculous.

The Jacksons were brilliant. There was little rush for us now. We enjoyed ourselves, meeting and chatting to all sorts of people who seemed fascinated to hear about our trip. The city centre was different to the Indian cities we had grown used to: it was smarter, with important looking office buildings and elegant shops. By the seafront there were lawns and gardens and the marine drive which ran alongside it was attractive.

But the people who walked the streets were much the same: a mixture of obvious government officials and businessmen, both Ceylonese and European, and that other group of "unexplainables". Only the money changers revealed their trade. You were rarely approached by the money changer himself; it was usually his runner who would carry out the negotiation. The runner, having asked the tourist if he had any hundred rupee Indian notes would continue: as "English Pound? English traveller cheque? Sixteen rupee, English pound ..." Since the official rate then was seven, this was attractive.

No sooner was our parting curry party with the Jacksons over than it was time for everybody to come down to the ship and see us off. These parties were always very popular ones in Ceylon for it gave everyone an opportunity to buy cheap drinks and cigarettes on board instead of paying the very high shore prices. The diary reads: "V.G. party – guests hardly got away in time, entire ship's company in a panic to get them off. Sailed just after 8. Said goodbye to Robin who must fly tomorrow lunchtime to London."

John and I were very sorry that Robin had to go home. We could scarcely have wished for a better travelling companion. He was tireless, decisive, useful, humorous, practical and strong. He was also the best tourist amongst us. He knew many points of interest that lay ahead and was soon on top of them. We had made a good trio: if two argued, the other looked bored and any quarrel would subside. He would be a big miss. Selfishly, we hoped, not a vital one.

We were not sure how the car would handle on return from the garage, but there was no chance to test it before loading. On the positive side, the engine and transmission had given us no trouble. The radiator had leaked because the battery had come away from its mounting and caused it to hole. We had travelled far beyond the capabilities of its suspension and chassis. It was bold and reckless of us to insist on a small family saloon, but it was fun and it made us friends along every road we travelled.

IX

Marooned in Aden

Our voyage over the Indian Ocean to Aden aboard *SS Strathnaver* took five-and-a-half days, with a call at Bombay. The steamship was one of the oldest in the P&O fleet and a year later would be in the breaker's yard. Our steward, Ellis, had sailed on her maiden voyage in 1931. He told us that it had only been kept in service this long because the Australia run was such a profitable one for the company. The service was luxurious by our standards. We met a few young people on board. There were many young Australians excited to be coming to Britain and an equal number of retired people who sat in deck chairs, consuming New Berry Fruits and sweet biscuits. The Boeing 707 jet had been in service for two years. Competition loomed.

At Bombay we went ashore looking for shipboard reading matter. The most entertaining was the Penguin edition of *The Dud Avocado* by Elaine Dundy. It had both John and I creased with laughter. It was hard to believe that we had left Bombay in the car only a fortnight before. Our stroll ended at our favourite milk bar, the Napoli, close by the Delamar Hotel. Recognised by the gang of small boys who had cleaned our car when we parked it outside, their faces dropped when they saw it was not with us. We wrote a card to Robin and rejoined the ship.

The passenger list had been swelled by a large number of Indians emigrating to England. We heard it said that if P&O only went as far as Bombay and forgot about Australia, they could fill their ships for twelve months of the year on the homeward journey.

At eight o'clock on Sunday 11 September we came up on deck to hear John play the haunting "Barren Rocks of Aden" on his bagpipes as those rocks shimmered before us in the early morning haze. We arrived in Aden with misgivings and real anxiety. At that time it was a British colony surrounded by the Aden Protectorate, ruled locally by tribal chiefs. This and Yemen to the north today occupy the south-western part of the massive Arabian peninsula – largely the land of Saudi Arabia. Oman lay to the east and along the southern coast. Yemen laid claim to Aden and would ultimately (in 1967) be successful in its embrace.

Mountains fringe the western and south-western coasts (including the Aden Protectorate). While Yemen had oil and a significant area of productive agricultural land, Aden possessed no oil and had few national resources. Its value as a colony was chiefly as a coaling station. It was the remotest British colony on the mainland.

Our intention was to cross the Red Sea to Massawa, Eritrea some 400 miles north up the East African coast and then enter Ethiopia, driving the length of that country into Kenya and then down to South Africa. This was a distance of around 7,000 miles, with some of the worst roads in the world in Ethiopia over the mountainous Great Rift Valley. Even for us this was a daunting prospect. Fewer ships from Aden crossed to Djibouti or Mombasa which would offer a more southerly starting point for our trip. There seemed no shorter alternatives.

It was strange that we felt further from home in Aden than ever we did in Colombo, although the distance was shorter. Perhaps this was because there we were "down the road", but in Aden, after a long sea passage by sea, we felt more remote. We were back in the land of *Time Magazine's* Atlantic edition; since Pakistan we had been reading the Pacific edition. Amongst other publications, it had kept us updated on the Kennedy–Nixon Election battle. None of this helped our sense of dilemma, marooned as we were in Aden.

Fortune, again, smiled on us. In no time and ashore we were to find friends, contacts, assistance, interest and even entertainment.

We had not disembarked before Martin Watts, the opposite number to P&O agent George Gater in Colombo, squeezed up the companionway to make contact. He would look for a ship to take us across the Red Sea, he told us after his welcome.

Landing at Steamer Point, we looked for a hotel. The rates were more expensive than in India, and we booked in at the Marina for under £2 a night. My tummy bug, evident on the ship, grew worse and my insides felt like an inflated balloon. None of Dr Hawtrey May's potions worked. The RAF doctor, Mason, at the Command Hospital had the answer – a two day cure. He prescribed some heinous drugs, one of which, when I took it, I thought must be poison and desperately felt the bottle for poison indicating corrugations. I collapsed on a chair for two minutes under its giddying effects. I was cured within two days though.

We found Aden had had a bad press. Our geography teachers had billed it merely as a coaling station and punishment posting. We found it a place of air conditioning; although 104 degrees Fahrenheit, it was a dry heat and certainly no worse than Iran or India. We liked Martin Watts not just for his air conditioning but also for his cold drinks and good company.

He found a Lloyd Triestino ship, the *SS Diana*, calling at Aden on Saturday bound for Massawa. It was now Monday. This was tight but possible.

Ron Cook, manager of National and Grindlays Bank, sent to Alfie Myers in Piccadilly to have him send £150 for our African drive. He had spent time in Africa and gave us good advice of this dark continent.

John made contact with the Royal Highland Fusiliers, with whom he had served his National Service in Malaya, who were stationed in Aden. His fine operational reputation stood us in good stead. He dined with them and they invited us to stay. They gave us total hospitality in their mess and made the time pass waiting for the ship more enjoyable than it might have been.

Nor was this the only military hospitality we enjoyed in the colony. Through my National Service in the Royal Marines, I made contact with some old acquaintances. I telephoned the colonel of 45 Commando Royal Marines where Dai Morgan, my troop commander during the Suez invasion, was staff officer. Dai had won the Military Cross at the Battle of the Garigliano River in Italy in 1943. I also got hold of Lieutenant Colonel Leslie Marsh who had won the Distinguished Service Order (DSO) in Korea as commanding officer. They were two fine soldiers and gave us a hilarious lunch.

I also had contact with an armoured cavalry regiment stationed there. They were less welcoming and took no notice of me at all when I visited! Meanwhile, John improved our stock at the Royal Highland mess by winning a drink tasting competition. The regiment had a 150 strong detachment at Mukeiras, 250 miles into the desert and 7,000 feet up in the mountains on the Yemeni border. We were invited to visit to our great interest and pleasure.

Aden Airways ran a twice daily Dakota DC-3 service into the village. Rising at half past four we caught the first plane. Our fellow passengers were locals, poultry and goats. Hens fluttered up and down the aisle throughout the flight while the goats wandered about. The terrain below us was rugged. Flat desert at first, then bare hills arose making the flight bumpy. As we came into land at Mukeiras, we saw, at the end of the runway, a crashed RAF Valletta transport. It was an isolated, wild location. The other way to approach Mukeiras was by donkey which made trade and communication difficult. A road was being blasted through, but this required engineering skills since the village stood at 7,000 feet. Land Rovers were provided but sand, rock and potholes shortened their lifespans to 5,000 miles. Perhaps our "small family saloon" was not so small after all!

At the camp, we met Major Dennis Halstead, the officer commanding the 157 strong detachment. He paid us the compliment of treating us seriously. He briefed us on the situation in those parts, introduced us to some of his officers and arranged a programme for our stay. He put us in the hands of Lieutenant Ian Cartwright, who took us into the village for a look around. It was a very simple one: the community pivoted on the square which itself was composed of mud buildings. There were a few shops in the square, the most important being the rifle shop. Here we were offered a Lee–Enfield, this time for £150 – nine times the £17 asked in the Pakistan tribal area seven weeks before.

Behind the village, on a small hill, a brick building was in the course of construction. This was to be a hotel, the first in Mukeiras. It was hard to believe there was trade to justify it, but Mukeiras was a resort town – the Brighton of Aden. It was cooler and a change from the coast. Close by stood the house of the naib, and Ian Cartwright went in with his interpreter to discover how it would be if we came to tea that afternoon. The naib, it appeared, was ill; he often was, we understood. But if we came back later in the day he might be gracious enough to meet and entertain us.

Our next visit was to Flight Lieutenant Ian Collins, the field intelligence officer, who was very much a lone operator. He lived outside the village. He had largely fitted it out for himself. The hot water system, for instance, came out of the crashed Valletta aircraft that we had seen on landing. Many said that he bragged too much but we found him interesting. Ian left us with him and, at first, he was somewhat reticent. But when he had found out that we were not reporters and were, in fact, enthralled by anything he had to tell us he relaxed. It was his job to obtain any information he could relating to activity on the Yemeni border. He had been over in Oman, but when transferred to Mukeiras he had managed to persuade the RAF to give him a reasonably free hand as to his methods. He never wore uniform, he lived away from all military establishments and had set himself up as a minor benefactor to the people, giving them medical advice and attention.

Sitting at his front porch, talking to him, we noticed an Arab mother and child approaching. "Her son has a burned arm and I am treating him," he volunteered after hailing them in Arabic. They sat down on the edge of the porch, and as he unwound the bandages they talked to each other in a friendly way.

Turning to us he said in English, "When I take this bandage off, you will notice that the child has an extra little finger. Don't remark upon it – it could easily be removed by tying some nylon thread tight around its base and letting it wither. But the people believe that it is the will of Allah that it is there and that it would be wrong to remove it." To us, looking at the sweet face of the child, and knowing that he would have to grow up with such a deformity, it seemed wrong not to remove it.

He gave the boy a sweet and the two returned to the village.

It was unfortunate that we were not staying longer, otherwise he could have arranged for us to visit the Yemen. By way of compensation, he had to visit a contact some miles away (on what business he declined to tell us) and he invited us to join him. Accompanied only by his faithful Arab signaller (who, we heard from another source, had once saved his life), and with the airy advice that if shot at en route we should carry on as if nothing had happened, we set off in his Land Rover. Physically, it was one uncomfortable motor ride. The vehicle, equipped with springs normally fitted to one ton trucks, made us feel every bump, and there were plenty of them. After two miles, we followed wadis and narrow tracks where we could and his nose if we could not. Ian Collins' nose was an able one, for we had soon lost all sense of direction and neither John nor I could have found our way back. His contact was not at home so we drove on to an escarpment from which the ground fell vertically away for 5,000 feet to the plain which led down to Aden. Coming up from below and to the left, we could hear the sounds of machinery that was driving the road through.

In the afternoon, it appeared that the naib was suffering from a bout of malaria but his cousin was kind enough to entertain us for tea. We were shown in and sat down to an English blended tea and TV biscuits! The cousin of the naib was a small man but imposing nonetheless. Across his middle he wore a belt from the centre of which hung a dagger, according to the local fashion. His, however, was no ordinary dagger and when we admired it he handed it to us to inspect. The handle was embossed with gold and exquisitely shaped, and the blade was very sharp indeed. He told us that he had once been to London; he had not been very impressed with it but had enjoyed riding on the Underground. We returned to the mountain base where we stayed overnight.

The next morning, Saturday 17 September, we flew back to Aden on board an RAF Beverley. This was the airfreight workhorse of the Royal Air Force. A huge box car, practical but slow, cruising at 130 mph. I had used it for parachute jumps in the past. We returned to find that the money we had ordered had arrived but the ship would not now arrive until Tuesday. The position was almost desperate: it seemed that even if we did not make the wedding in Johannesburg, we were still going to be very rushed to arrive in time for John's plane which was leaving a week later.

Dennis Halstead had also flown down from Mukeiras for the day and we told him of our difficulty. "Hmm," he said, "how darned annoying." Then he brightened: "Why not try the RAF?"

"The RAF?" we queried.

"Yes, they often fly Beverley transports over to Nairobi, either completely empty or carrying less than their payload, and they always help if they can. I tell you what, I'll get in touch with the duty movements officer and see what they can do."

"That would be most kind," we replied, "but do they ever fly over to Addis Ababa?" We still wanted include Ethiopia.

"I don't know, but I will ask them," he replied patiently.

He telephoned and discovered that there was a flight

leaving on Monday for Nairobi below its payload and that we may be able to get aboard. Further enquiries revealed that it was unlikely that we would be able to get a flight to Ethiopia, so if we still wanted to go we would have to go on the *Diana*. Thus, we had to make the reluctant decision to sacrifice Ethiopia. It proved a wise one. The car was fragile: if any proof were needed of this, and it certainly was not, we broke down six times in our first four days after landing in Kenya, even on roads surely better than in Ethiopia, and in a country where it was possible to obtain mechanical aid without too much difficulty.

The decision had had to be taken: John could not risk being late in taking up his job in De Havilland's at Hatfield. But at this stage it was no use talking in too concrete terms for we were not yet sure of our flight. Ethiopia would have made the end of our trip a fiasco. In the evening, through a contact, I was invited to dinner at the officer's mess of the Queen's Own Hussars who were stationed in Aden to provide support for the Royal Highland Fusiliers. I discovered how lucky we were to be staying with the Royal Highland Fusiliers. They did not make me welcome. They took no interest in our travels and discouraged any conversational initiative on my part. Regiments differ and we had been fortunate with John's.

The next day, John telephoned again but the duty officer had changed, and it being Sunday, there was nobody in authority to whom we could speak. However, things still seemed hopeful and the next day, by dint of some talking and a little persuading, John fixed the flight for early on Tuesday morning. As reservist officers, we were to be allowed to fly (my commission had been gazetted only a week before leaving) and we were to take the car to RAF Khormaksar that afternoon to be drained of petrol prior to loading. I could not believe our luck, for it was almost beginning to look as though John would have to return home from Aden; but I would not believe it until we were airborne.

The new plan of flying to Nairobi involved backpedalling on our previous one. First, we went to see Martin Watts to tell him. He was doubtful about us getting our money back from the shipping company. So, for the last time, we went out of his office, into the wall of heat, through some railings, across the baking football pitch, through some more railings, across the street and into another oasis of air conditioning, the National and Grindlays Bank. We spoke to Ron Cook and changed the extra Ethiopian dollars we had bought back into East African shillings.

That afternoon, we drove to RAF Khormaksar, drained the car of petrol and left it with the authorities. All that remained to be done was to attempt to recover our fare to Ethiopia. The shipping office was at Crater, a township some two miles inland. It is so called because it is situated in a crater, with the result that it can become more uncomfortably hot than Aden itself. It was around the sides of this crater that huge water catchments would trap the rain when it came and provide water for the community.

At the shipping office we were shown into the manager's office, and he turned out to be an ex-Christ's College, Cambridge man. By dint of this and some persuasion, we were able to recover our money and thus made a considerable saving. The RAF carried ourselves, our kit, the car, the works, all for a five and sixpenny messing charge each (28p). As one commentator remarked of our tale, "That was extremely civil of them." Very civil, we thought, for 1,200 miles over the Red Sea and Ethiopia.

Martin Watts, Morton Pollock and John Edwardes were our guests at dinner that night at the Galleon Grill. They had been good to us: Martin had guided us from first to last while Morton and John had been terrific friends and hosts.

It was a late night, so it was not surprising that we didn't hear our five o'clock alarm and had to be shaken awake at ten minutes to six. We need not have worried. The doors of the Beverley aircraft in which we were to fly had jammed and we spent forty-five minutes on tenterhooks thinking that the flight would be cancelled and our plans laid at nought once more. When, at last, we did take off we needed the entire runway to do it, so heavily laden was the aircraft. Splendid RAF – they had stretched the flight to the limit to carry us. Our luck had held from Trichinopoly to RAF Eastleigh, Nairobi, a passage of twenty-four days. We had seventeen left until the wedding.

I looked down directly over Ethiopia and thought of the bitter driving that we had missed over that barren land. I thought of the three months we had spent in Asia and on the ocean that embraced us. I moved to the cockpit and talked to the navigator – Blank Africa stretched before us and beneath us. One might think that Asia had more in common with Africa than Europe, but not so. Europe and Asia are heavily populated in every area where habitation seems possible; and in places like Baluchistan where it was not, every patch where a grain of rice or husk of corn could grow was cultivated. By contrast, Africa was a spacious and clean continent. The frustration of Africa is that there is room for everyone, if only they would live together.

X

Africa

We touched down at three in the afternoon. The customs were no worry as the only official on duty was just going off to have his tea. Unloading took longer: two large crates of aircraft spares lay in front of the car and since the only forklift truck was out of order, they had to be unloaded by hand. We sat in the customs hut, chatting to any passers through who cared to talk to us.

We were told that labour is cheap in theory but not in practice in Kenya; that it takes six men to do a one man job; that in a recent railway strike the staff were reduced from their usual 17,000 to 5,000 persons, with the result that the railways made a profit for the first time in their history; that Earl Mountbatten was to fly in that evening; and that many members of the English press were about to report his visit and investigate the doings of British troops in the area, with the result that as many troops as was prudently possible had been despatched on location to conduct small scale exercises and thus grant themselves some sort of *raison d'être* in the colony. The real reason for such concentration as there was (in addition, the 42 Commando carrier was lurking just over the Mombasa horizon) was a belief that a native rising might be in the offing. Yet another loquacious informant opined that although Kenya was slipping, it would be some time before the British were kicked out altogether. The opinion that impressed us most, however, was that we should be able to get tea in the local officers' mess, and by the time we had done this our car was ready to drive into Nairobi.

It was night. Our efforts to find a bed were at first unrewarding. The YMCA sounded a good bet. I asked a man in a bar with a badge on his blazer where it was, but he was so offended at the thought that I might be thinking he was the type of man who would visit such a place that he wouldn't tell me. When we finally found it, the manager only offered us two beds in a dormitory, which was not good enough for us with all our equipment to safeguard, so we resigned ourselves to the luxury of the Grosvenor Hotel. Whether it was the hotel or the sight of Nairobi in the morning that gave us the impression, I don't know, but I noted in the diary next morning that Nairobi was "quite an impressive city and the most civilised and sophisticated we have seen since Europe".

We soon calculated that in British Africa then, amongst all peoples, the discontented far outnumbered the contented. The days of paradise and the feeling of endless space that had enchanted so many from Britain (much encouraged by the British government) were over. This brought John and I much sadness and regret.

Once more, we felt the water would be drinkable and garages reliable. The Austin agent in Nairobi was more than reliable. I had a friend there, Horace Gow, with whom I had served in the Royal Marines. Strangely, by means of some sixth sense, I had been expecting to meet him on the trip somewhere, and now I had.

Our car was ready and its battery charged. We lost no time in driving out of town to the Royal Nairobi National Park. At that time, wild beasts and a vision of Africa in its almost original state were to be found only three miles outside Nairobi's boundaries. We saw our first lions there, the only ones that we were to see in Africa: a mother lion with three cubs, relaxing, yawning and licking each other in the long grass. They took little notice of us; not ignoring us but taking us for granted, rather like domestic cats. We saw many other animals as well – giraffes, ostriches, impala. It was here that we first regretted our form of transport, for our Austin A40 now became a burden and restricted our freedom of movement. With a Land Rover, we would have had no trouble roaming over the bush at will. As it was, the A40 was in a parlous state and was to become more fragile still before we climbed the hill to Johannesburg. We had to be extremely careful to reconnoitre the ground before we took it off the main track.

Zul Kassim-Lakha was a friend of John Maclay from St John's College, Cambridge whose father owned a large hotel in Kampala. The capital of Uganda is built on seven hills lying twenty miles north of the crocodile-infested Lake Victoria from whose waters flow the Nile at Jinja and upon whose banks stands Entebbe, the old capital, the town with the international airport and the residence of the governor-general. By manipulating our schedule, we deemed that we had a sufficient period in hand to accept Zul's invitation and still be in Johannesburg on 8 October. We had missed Ethiopia, so we could partially make up for that by an expedition to Uganda. Accordingly, we set out the next morning, Thursday 22 September. Our route was Nairobi, Nanyuki, passing by Mount Kenya (at 4,500 feet), Nakuru, Eldoret to Kampala – some 450 miles.

But what of Robin all this time? We had been to Uganda and were far south of Nairobi and in Tanganyika

(Tanzania) by the time we were able to write him a letter. Naturally, it was a breakdown that afforded us the opportunity. I reproduce it here, not only because it provides the best description of events to that point, but because I think it may capture for the reader some of the sense of the spirit of a rapid expedition like ours.

Station Hotel
Dodoma, Tanganyika
September 29th, 1960

Dear Robin,

Day 98, Thursday, September 22nd

Set off north from Nairobi towards the Mount Kenya district. Not 50 miles out of town before the right shock absorber gave way, two bolts having sheared. C got a lift back to Thika, the nearest town, from a chap who had been on a 5 day fishing jaunt. Had been a volunteer during the war, having seen service out here in the Abyssinian campaign, he had been attracted and he came out in 1948. Came from Abingdon but could not stand England's crowds. Had all he wanted in Kenya, managed a coffee farm. C got the parts at first try, then an immediate lift back by someone who was working on the road project down by our collapsed car. The break caused 3 hours delay, then we spent another hour, as invited, "having a noggin at the Nog Inn". The chap there was a retired school master who also ran a 1000 acre farm. He said the workers' union, not the workers themselves, wanted more pay, he would be delighted to grant this for a full day's work, but they all like to start at 7 a.m. and about 11.30 a.m. go off and sleep or till their own little plots of land.

Left him after a very cheap steak lunch (food very cheap out here seven shillings/ (30p) for a meal that would cost twice as much in the UK), went on to Nyeri where the great Tree Tops Hotel is £10 a night (see game or your money back). Sent you a telegram from here for the exams.

Drove on to Nanyuki, dominated by the snow-capped Mount Kenya. Both Nanyuki and Mount Kenya (5199 m) stand precisely on the equator. The roads by now are dirt with potholes, sometimes corrugated but allow a fair 40/50 speed. At Nanyuki were the 3rd King's African Rifles with whom is one of John's army chums who, in fact, was in Nairobi at the time. Stayed in the local hotel: "The Sportsman's Arms" – full of old army colonels – very depressing. As we parked the car, all the electrics of the car failed – a problem for the morning!

Day 99, Friday, September 23rd

Upped and round the garage (the electrics had picked up again) and they traced it to the ammeter. We should never have fitted one. Just about to drive off when up comes Sam Small, a local American settler, who, typically American, wanted us to have a beer, see round his 6,000 acres, stay the

week in quick succession. We went off
to have a beer at the local club. He told
us that he had come out from Baltimore
("You've really heard of that?") 3 years
ago to help his asthma, he was staying
whatever the politicians, black or white,
did. Was in a steel firm before and in the
British Commandos during the war. Told
us of the enormous troop concentrations
and movements out here – 24 Brigade, the
commando carrier *HMS Bulwark* was at
Mombasa, Lord Mountbatten had just flown
out (the day before we arrived) to observe a
brigade movement from the UK. This is the
big centre for any African flare-up from the
British point of view. To give up Kenya, he
says, along with many others, is to hand it
over to the Russians. He pressed us to stay,
but we had plans to go to Kampala and stay
with Zul Kassim-Lakha there.

We said goodbye at noon and set off –
terrible road across to Nakuru which would
put us on the main Nairobi–Kampala road.
We negotiated the powerful mountains of
the Rift Valley as we went. Journey was
not without casualty and soon the leading
shackle on one of the rear springs was
broken, binding the brakes. Loosened them
off, reached Nakuru, got things mended
there by 5.30. Meanwhile we took a taxi
to the local lake to see the flamingos which
are the great local attraction. Quite rightly
so, they are beautiful pink things with black
undersides to their wings. They paddle by

the side of the lake, huge squadrons of them all together. Whole sections of the lake are made pink by them. When they take off, they do so in a drilled, wheeling affine formation like a giant leaf from a tree.

We collected the car and made the next town, Eldoret, about 100 miles further up the road. Stayed in a hotel again. It was a very lonely place. Chris once met a retired colonial officer whose first posting had been there. He told him that he filled his time translating the bible into the local language. Unsung people provide such wholesome dedication.

Day 100, Saturday, September 24th

Drove on into Uganda – tarmac at once after crossing the border (only a driving licence check at the border). Kenya did not have enough money after the Mau Mau trouble with which to tarmac their roads. Also the Ugandan countryside was much greener and more fertile. More trouble on the road, this time a defective back axle oil seal and oil was leaking, also we discovered that the other leading shackle on the rear had broken. We rang Zul from a place called Bugiri and told him we would be late since we had to drive slowly. We met him for a late lunch at his father's Imperial Hotel.

After this, we sought out a garage, difficult on a Saturday afternoon. Finally, we tracked down a ropey old place run by two

Sikhs, who said they would do the job so we left them to it. Kampala is neither as sophisticated nor developed as Nairobi, but it is expanding rapidly with tall buildings and ambitious schemes. It has a population of 100,000 compared to Nairobi's quarter of a million. Both cities sprawl over the place. Kampala is very proud of the fact that it is built on seven hills – one would have been enough. Entebbe was the original capital, Government House and much of the secretariat are still there, but the new Uganda Parliament Buildings along with other administrative institutions are in Kampala. Zul and his brother, Amir, showed us around town. We bought some African arts and crafts figures, then we went to collect the car. All seemed fixed ok – we were soon to learn better. Back to dinner, the Kassim-Lakhas are a charming family. Afterwards we went out for drink but the town was rather dead.

Day 101, Sunday, September 25th

Went down to Entebbe. We visited Government House which had a beautiful situation overlooking the crocodile infested Lake Victoria. This, the second largest lake in the world in terms of surface area, provides head water for the Nile. Went to the airport. We saw a De Havilland Comet, the first of the jet airliners, take off. It was handsome, and John, soon to join the company, was proud. Back to Kampala. An overall 55 mph speed limit in Uganda, so a constant watch for police. Driving was fairly easy in Uganda but we were told that native drivers and pedestrians were a constant danger. In Kampala, farewells to Zul and family, so kind. They supplied us with a packed lunch and we bowled off down the road doing 100 miles in the first two hours on the tarmac. At Jinja, the first town down the road, the headwaters of the Nile are controlled. Owen Falls is the name of the location on the river.

Into Kenya, and onto the rough again, the steering went awry and oh! if we didn't have a wheel about to come off. That garage hadn't secured it properly. The wheel was wrecked but we put on a spare and if that didn't have a puncture within 20 miles! Incidentally, by this time the back axle was again leaking oil. This was all until we got back to Nairobi but 6 breakdowns in 4 days we thought excessive.

Reached Nakuru and the tarmac once more 92 miles from Nairobi. 10 o'clock, but we decided to make Nairobi that night. These 92 miles are twisty only in parts but have some straight stretches. We heard that a Aston Martin DB4 did the journey in 46 minutes – a local record. However, the police speed trap caught him through a village and he was fined £200. Another trick they have to slow motorists out here is to dig up railway crossings – quite a good idea, in fact, most effective.

Returned to our nice hotel in Nairobi just after midnight, 407 miles in 10 hours, excluding stops, not bad we reckoned. Nobody will look at an A40 out here. The Austin people in Nairobi told us, without prompting, that the springs break up, the doors rattle to pieces and are likely to spring open in awkward places.

Day 102, Monday, September 26th

Breakfasted over the *East African Standard*, quite the best overseas English newspaper we have come across so far, with a real international reportage; much better than the *Times of India* etc. Got the car in for a service and oil seal repair – apparently the Sikhs had put the oil seal in back to front. Zul's cousin, Sharush, showed us all around Nairobi in the morning including the place where they make Meerschaum pipes, the only other place outside Turkey. Had lunch, collected the car, drove south into Tanganyika.

Snow-capped and extinct Mount Kilimanjaro (5895 m) dominated to our left. It is Africa's highest mountain. This was real motoring, man, impalas running across the road in front of you, ostriches strutting alongside while the odd giraffe looked on as we passed. A cloud of vultures ahead, and there was a dead elephant by the roadside, its tusks missing due to poachers. At Arusha, we stayed at the New Safari Hotel. Loads of Americans there, all film technicians.

Shortly, John Wayne and others are to fly in to start shooting a film, *Attari*, and is to be about poaching on a game reserve. Shooting game is expensive out here. It costs £100 for a licence to shoot *one* elephant. When C made a remark at the bar about it having an atmosphere somewhat like that of a dude ranch, there were lots of dirty looks and one American moved off in disgust! We took the opportunity to write the loads of thank you letters that we owed, then went to bed.

Day 103, Tuesday, September 27th

Drove further south, visited Ngorongoro Crater where there is said to be more game than anywhere else in Africa. We were unfortunate and did not see anything. Stopped at a village, bought some things for supper and camped down 20 miles from the main road which we left in order to visit the crater.

Day 104, Wednesday, September 28th

We had coffee, bread and butter for breakfast, struck camp, no bills, no tips to pay – wonderful! Discovered jack was missing, heaven knows where that went – good excuse to get rid of it anyway, but let us hope we reach Dodoma, Tanganyika's largest and most central town, nearly 250 miles away, without mishap.

We did not. 500 yards down the road the brakes jammed on and the leading shackle had gone again, they would not release themselves without the wheel being raised. Along came a truck, and, shamefully, we asked him for a jack. He produced a beautiful hydraulic one, a joy to behold – if only we had had one of those all along. John was able to loosen the brakes and we drove on. It took us all day to reach Dodoma, the roads were terrible but the scenery fairly pleasant with some beautiful browns and greens in the trees. Quaint cacti grew on the hillsides.

We went to the police station on arrival and got permission to camp in the police yard. Then we went to the hotel to have a bath, have dinner (we had had nothing all day) and to read in motor manufacturers' magazines how an Austin 7 drove to Prague and back, an A40 to Switzerland, a Triumph Herald to God knows where – all without the slightest spot of bother, and giving mpg rates correct to at least 9 places of decimals. We also met someone who was in the Royal Engineers in Kenya – had attempted to hitchhike to Rhodesia, his old home, within a month's leave, but the going had been too slow for him to make it.

We went back to the police station where we pitched the tent, chased away the mosquitoes, and went to sleep.

Day 105, Thursday, September 29th

Woke up to a beautiful day. Took the car to a garage. John now spotted that the other leading shackle had gone again, so it goes on, the whole of the bottom of the car is breaking up.

Hope all has gone well with the exams.

Yours,

John and Christopher

While I sat in Dodoma writing to Robin, John was down at the garage chivvying and advising the mechanics. He came back with the news that the shackles and their fixings had received such a bashing that the bodywork around their bases was breaking up and the garage was having to build this up again with pieces of steel plate. Some of the jobs that John persuaded these garages to do, English garages would hardly have looked at, and perhaps may not have had the ability to repair them. It turned out that John had done the business this time. We were to have a much better result. At least it seemed that we had been fortunate in our choice of garage.

It was sunset and the car was ready. We set off into the increasing southern dusk. The roads were as terrible as ever. John insisted that we travelled dead slow, 20 mph, picking our way through the potholes. Attracted by the glare of our headlights, impala poked their slim bodies out of the dense bush and then darted back again as we went by. At two in the morning, two or three miles before we reached that night's target, Iringa, the next town, we at last found a break in the bush, halted, set up our beds and sleeping bags, and went to sleep.

We awoke to see an air sock flapping in the morning sun, and an African urgently talking to us in Swahili. Another African approached us to say the same in English – that an aircraft was expected within the half hour and we were on the runway! No bureaucrats these,

On the Road

Caspian Robin: Robin shows his sense of humour as he proffers a sample of our consistent diet of Fray Bentos steak and kidney pie with his back to the Caspian beach. The sea here is the world's largest body of inland water with an area bigger than that of Great Britain.

John making the first breakfast near Nancy, France. Note the use of the front seats of the car adapted for use as camping stools.

Central India was flooded with monsoon water, as this road illustrates.

Caspian John: John ponders how to repair the car's hydraulic clutch to drive it from the Caspian's 90 feet below sea level over the 9,000 foot pass to Tehran and mechanical help.

A large truck stuck beneath the superstructure of a bridge in eastern Turkey forced us to make a detour along the old Soviet border and Mount Ararat to reach the Iranian border.

First trial for our 'Casino' tent: plenty of height, easy entrance.

A Tabriz (Iran) real family business as grandfather, son and grandson make ready to mend our rear suspension.

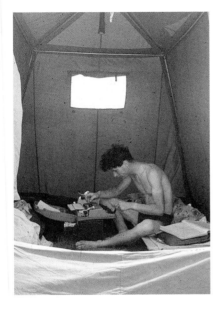

Caspian Chris: Christopher wrote the diary and letters home to be distributed by his father's secretary Linda Marshall.

John has his pipes bid farewell to eastern Turkey.

Dual-purpose toilet paper.

'I don't think so Chris'. Bartholomew's Maps and full discussion kept us on the correct road.

Ali Tobraki introduced us to a lot of people in Tabriz.

Wykehamists are everywhere! John meets some old school friends in Iran.

Africa

We had the RAF to thank for transport from Aden to Nairobi.

The Border Post between Tanganyika and Northern Rhodesia. Despite both countries being British Colonies, it proved the most awkward. The Officer demanded a deposit of £150 for transit through the country.

The grand Kariba Dam.

The mighty Zambesi harnessed.

The charming Kassim Lakhas who hosted us in Kampala. They were later expelled by Idi Amin and their glorious Kampala hotel forfeited to the state of Uganda.

Kissing the road as we reached Nakuru, Kenya and asphalt surface resumed.

On the equator.

The roadside menagerie made our African drive both lively and superb.

Victoria Falls: The force of the Zambesi made the water spout over the rocky brink before falling below.

thank heavens, and the amusement was shared by all. We moved off the airfield and they showed us to a shed where there was a tap and other washing facilities. In Iringa, we ate a typically massive East African breakfast, bought an excellent hydraulic jack and some food to last us the day before we reached the border, after Mbeya. Our morale which had been sagging the day before was restored.

Travel was as slow as the night before but we made Mbeya before sundown, albeit in a thunderstorm. The next day we had the car serviced and the oil changed so we were not away until a quarter to eleven, but we reached the border town of Nakonde some seventy miles south shortly before two. At the Tanganyika–Rhodesia customs post, an Indian represented Tanganyika and an Englishman Northern Rhodesia. The Tanganyikan Indian official was upset that we had not reported our presence in the country. Nobody had told us to do so. Nor could we produce an East African sixpence as a stamp fee since we had purposely used up all our spare change when we filled up with petrol.

The Rhodesian English official required either a return ticket to England or £150 in cash as security in Rhodesian money. John found his air ticket, but I had neither Rhodesian cash nor a ticket. He was being awkward and deathly polite at the same time, obviously enjoying it all. Nobody had told us of these requirements.

He insisted that the money was in Rhodesian currency, of which we had not a penny, and he would not accept traveller's cheques. In any case, we were not sure that all our currency of any denomination would add up to £150. We offered to go to the bank to change the money. "The nearest bank is 600 miles away, sir," he blocked. We offered to telephone the bank to see if they could suggest anything. "Where are you going to telephone from, sir? The nearest telephone is 50 miles away."

In that hostile customs house we seemed to have one friend. His opposite number on the Tanganyikan side who seemed to share our dislike of his counterpart. He gave us the name of an Indian in the village who might have the necessary cash. We trekked up the hill to the village but he did not. By the expression on the customs officer's face when we returned, it seemed he knew that we would fail.

The situation was critical. We would have to cancel our visit to the Copperbelt in Northern Rhodesia (Zambia), and the way things were looking we would have to bump seventy miles back to Mbeya for the weekend. When we had asked in Rhodesia House in London before our departure about border procedure, they mentioned nothing of this deposit requirement.

"Of course, if you could prove that you were a bona fide student, I could let you through for £100," the customs officer intimated. I produced a letter on headed writing paper from my tutor at Cambridge. It wished us luck for the trip. "No, this won't do, sir." We finally compromised on £130, but in Rhodesian money. All seemed lost but then our Indian friend found a joker in the pack. He gave us the name of another of his commercial contacts in the village and handed us a note for him saying, "Please change all money and traveller's cheques". His name was Mr Sen Joshi, a saint if ever there was one. Note in hand, we set off once more up the steep quarter mile hill.

Mr Joshi was just off to Broken Hill (a town 600 miles south in Northern Rhodesia) with the village sweepstake funds. He held up the bus, sat down at the desk in his little shop and listened to our story.

"OK," he said, "I see you are in a feex. Since you are in a feex I will help you – my credit is good. If you deceive me, I lose, but your credit is not good; my credit is good. That is my Indian philosophy." "Three cheers for Indian philosophy," we thought. So saying, Mr Joshi reached for the sweepstake funds and asked us to dictate the rates of exchange that we had written on a Gestetner duplicated sheet given to us by Mr Myers of the Midland Bank before we left. He refused Ethiopian dollars but he changed pound notes, traveller's cheques, French francs (old and new), American dollars, German marks and, if you please, Austrian schillings, of which he had probably never heard. The total was £142, leaving us £12 to reach the 600 miles to the Copperbelt. Thanking Mr Joshi profusely, we returned to the customs house trying to look as miserable as possible, having stuffed the wads of notes into our pockets. I must confess that we tried to lead the customs officer up the garden path, once again asking for a waiver which we knew he would not give us. We chatted to him for a further five minutes until he was firmly convinced that we had again been foiled. Then, confirming that the price was £130, refundable on exit, so that he could not go back on his word, we pulled out the money stuffed in our pockets. We had begun to suspect that his little tricks were well known in the village and disapproved of.

He stared at us in dismay. "Right, sign here," he snapped, jerking a paper over to us. We gladly did and, bidding farewell to our erstwhile captor, and a fonder one for our Indian ally, we set off on the dusty road to the Copperbelt of Northern Rhodesia. It had been a close shave.

Anthony Kenny was a very good university friend of mine. His father ran the Mufulira copper mine, the largest in Rhodesia, for Anglo American. His parents had asked us to stay. To maintain our schedule we decided that we must drive overnight to arrive there the following morning. Going from Tanganyika into Rhodesia, as far as the roads were concerned, was like going from Persia into Pakistan: no more potholes. The surface was still dusty and corrugated but only severely so on the bends; we were thus able to make excellent progress at just over 40 mph. At ten o'clock we had dinner at Mpika, 150 miles further on, and just as dawn was breaking, we hit the asphalt at Kapiri Mposhi, filled up at an all-night garage and turned right up the road to Ndola and the Copperbelt. I slept over much of this stretch and was woken by John shouting, "Fifty miles in fifty minutes!" We had never done that, even on the Autobahn.

XI

Champagne and Velvet Roads

We parked in front of the Rhodes Hotel, Ndola, the centre of the Copperbelt, and behind a Land Rover bearing the inscription, "Trans-Africa 1960", whose owner, unfortunately, we did not have the opportunity of meeting. Inside, we had a bath and ordered breakfast, which was a repast as large as any served in East Africa. We rang Mr Kenny who told us that Mrs Kenny was away in Durban, but asked us to his house in Mufulira, several miles west of Ndola.

He drove us around the mine area, telling us a little of the commercial and political situation as he did so. At that time there was a good deal of trouble in the Congo, and the Katanga border was less than twenty miles away. The central African Copperbelt was one of the richest copper producing areas in the world. It had, however, two main drawbacks. First, location: the distance from the world markets was much greater than any other such area, the nearest being 5,000 miles away. Furthermore, the mines were well inland and rail routes to the sea could be politically unreliable. The usual route for copper was by the railway running through Congo and Angola to the port of Lobito Bay, but at the time we were there this way was closed and the mineral was having to be taken to Lourenço Marques in Portuguese East Africa (now Mozambique).

Great strides were being made. In the past two or three years, output per man had been doubled and it was hoped to double it again in the next three years.

Labour was not all that cheap; by African standards wages were extremely high and conditions very good. The Africans had a great desire to work to improve their status and capabilities. Some 12,000 workers were employed at the mine, with between 400 and 500 of them earning more than £1,000 a year (I did not have such an income in England until 1962). The basic minimum wage was £15 a month. As for conditions, many new dwellings had been built and more were under construction. One trouble, we were told, with raising wages, which the company was anxious to do, was that although this was all right up to a point, after a time the extended family would discover how well their relative was doing at the mine and come and live off him. To control these problems, and to attempt to sort them out, the organisation kept a large personnel department: forty-five to look after the Africans and twenty to look after the Europeans.

There was ill feeling against the British for the way they had handled the Central African situation. Many felt that they had been sold out. There were complaints too of a lack of understanding, particularly with regard to racial problems, when they felt they were doing so much to better the Africans' standard of living. Parliamentary and other delegations came out sniffing for trouble and took back unfairly adverse reports. They had been pleased with the most recent arrivals from the House of Commons, though, for they had actually liked what they saw. One man, who had relatives in Chester-le-Street, County Durham, spoke disparagingly to me of the adverse slum conditions in the north of England, and suggested that although I might think the Africans were accommodated in grass huts, many actually lived in better housing than people in certain parts of the north-east of England. Indeed, we were told of the struggle to persuade African workers to live in the modern huts built for them. But the Rhodesians had survived much better than the Europeans from the Congo. Just before the Congolese revolt the Kennys had offered hospitality to thirty friends from the Congo should the need arise. Twenty-seven had taken up the offer.

Having lunched with Mr Kenny, we drove to the airstrip with him to see him fly off to Salisbury (Harare) to the meeting would to decide to cut back copper production by ten per cent, while maintaining the same labour force, and thus keep the price of copper at £230 per ton. We then toured Luanshya, home of the Roan Antelope mine, and Kitwe. Returning to Mufulira, we were admirably and courteously looked after by Major Townsend, Mr Kenny's personal assistant. He was one of many members of the Indian Army who, at independence, had crossed the Indian Ocean to take up a life in Africa.

We made up for the lost sleep that night and awoke the next day, refreshed, for a tour of Mufulira, the largest mine in the Copperbelt. We were introduced to a mine captain, a highly responsible man who looked after a 200 foot section of the seam. Before the descent, we talked to him and some of his colleagues in the office. Dressed in rubber boots, overalls and helmets, we descended 1,150 feet to the first seam, which was almost worked out. At 1,400 feet, the main working level, we left the lift. Hard rock mining means much blasting and little pit-propping, quite unlike coal mining. Where pit-propping is required, however, the pressures are so enormous that only solid steel "I" sections, like railway lines, are strong enough. If wood is used, only Oregon timber (one of the hardest woods in the world) will suffice, but even this begins to crack after a few weeks and has to be replaced. The main labour force was African, closely supervised by Europeans – not only English but also Poles, Hungarians and others.

The principle of mining copper is quite simple: blast out the rock, then make the pieces as small as possible so the maximum amount of material can be put in the "skips" or carts and carried along the underground railway to the lift. The first stage in making the rock smaller is the "grizzley", a long, rectangular, steel-lined hole. These orifices are situated at intervals along the length of the seam being worked. Things are managed such that whenever the rock is blasted, the debris falls towards the grizzley. Those chunks that are small enough fall at once through the grizzley to the level below, while the rest remains above. Workers and supervisors alike then chain themselves to the face using hooks and chains, and set to with levers and picks to force the rest of that darned rock through the hole to the level below.

A previous visitor to the mine had been Mrs Barbara Castle. She had misunderstood the safety chains and had shocked many by returning to England to announce that African miners were chained captive to the rock face. I never saw this particular story in the press, but this is what we were told out there. They were sensitive and felt picked on.

We departed, and that afternoon we drove further south. The car was going well and we were putting sixty miles behind us in an hour. The roads were empty and, on this stage, fully asphalted. Driving was very safe.

We wanted to visit the two great sites of the Zambesi River: the Kariba Dam and Victoria Falls. This could not be done with one direct route; it meant passing through Northern Rhodesia's capital, Lusaka, taking a left fork east to Kariba, visiting the dam, then retracing our route and taking the right fork west down to Victoria Falls and finally crossing the Zambesi into Southern Rhodesia (Zimbabwe). We took an evening meal at a Cypriot Restaurant in Lusaka. The manager had been at the Ktima Gymnasium (or grammar school) in Cyprus when I had been there during my National Service. The school had always been a centre for anti-British rebellion but we got on well enough.

We took the left fork and camped amongst some roadside trees around forty miles from Kariba. On a lovely, still moonlit night, we set up our beds some way off the road. After a few jests about elephant trails and other signs of savage life that we had pretended to have found to scare one another, we fell asleep under the African starlight. It was a fine, if foolhardy, experience.

The Kariba Dam is 300 miles downstream from the Victoria Falls. The Zambesi then flows east into Mozambique. The blockage of the dam has caused Lake Kariba to fill. The Kariba Dam was a magnificent construction – timeless, comparable in architectural and scenic worth with Roman aqueducts. It was indeed built by Roman successors: Impresit, the Italian contractors. The spectacle was only marred for us by the sight under our motor car, as John discovered that yet another leaf spring had broken. It was back to Lusaka for us before we could get a replacement, so another upset to our schedule, and we did not see the Victoria Falls until the following morning.

We had met a pram salesman the previous evening who claimed that he could piss stronger than the Victoria Falls at that season. When we finally saw them we realised that he must be inordinately productive at that particular function or, more likely, he'd had a bad week with the prams. What is so striking is the force with which the water comes over the top of the waterfall. The mighty Zambezi has such pressure to start with that it does not just fall or flop over, the water comes spouting down. The falls are over a mile broad and rush into a huge gorge. There was a soaking spray. It was good that the sun was hot enough to dry us out quickly. A fine sculpture of Livingstone stands close by.

Southern Rhodesian roads generally had a central asphalt strip and dirt margins. It must have been on one of the detours that we sheared a front shackle pin again. This led to the further discovery that the Lusaka garage, when stripping the leaves, had replaced only eight of them, not ten. The garage in Wankie (now known as Hwange) had given up the Austin agency as they did not receive an adequate spares service, so we went to the garage that had taken it on, but they did not have the shackle pin required. As often happens in such cases, we were able to obtain the part at an unassuming garage in a small settlement further down the road and fit it ourselves. We dined after this and again met our pram salesman friend. We camped a few miles north of Bulawayo. Wankie was important as a coal mining town.

Everyone in Bulawayo reads *The Chronicle*, and a woman reporter from this paper saw our car and had us photographed for the paper. The other journalists were surprised to hear us praise Rhodesian roads; indeed, they were running a campaign for their improvement. All life is relative. Most of the paper concerned itself with farming topics and, on the political side, with the South African referendum results as to whether or not the Union should become a republic. This was the season of the jacaranda blossoms. We had their mass of pink blooms all the way from the Copperbelt to Pretoria, most memorably as we drove out of Bulawayo through a long avenue of them. We found Southern Rhodesia to be a most agreeable place, and can only regret that it is now run by those incapable of controlling a society by consent.

Beitbridge is the border town leading into South Africa. It stands on the River Limpopo, and it was a very fast run over a good road from Bulawayo. After our experiences with the Northern Rhodesian customs, we had some misgivings about our reception here. In the event, everybody was extremely pleasant, even humorous. We had our hard-fought deposit returned at once with no questions asked. South Africa demanded no such deposit. When they had to charge a small amount for some official service, they did not quibble over accepting Rhodesian change, saying, "Give us anything you like, so long as you don't boycott us."

The gate swung open to allow us through into the Union of South Africa. With relief we drove through and it shut behind us; we were over our last frontier. Johannesburg was less 300 miles to the south. We planned to reach it the next day – the eve of the wedding. We covered 200 of those that afternoon and evening.

That night found us in a motel about 150 miles from Johannesburg. Early the next day we has reached Pretoria, and looked around the government buildings and the Voortrekker Monument. This was oblong shaped and not a particularly pretty construction. Inside were a series of bas-reliefs illustrating the history of Voortrekkers, ending with one showing them being thrown out of Natal by the British.

Pretoria is one of the country's four capital cities. It lies thirty miles short of Johannesburg and serves as the seat of the executive branch of government. Cape Town is the legislative capital, Bloemfontein the judicial capital and Johannesburg is the home of the Constitutional Court.

We reached Johannesburg the same day. We went to stay with John's Aunt Louise, Mrs Young. She soon had our washing organised and put us in a bath. She set a pattern for the entertainment and hospitality we were to receive throughout our time in South Africa. We had arrived at drinks time on the "stoep", as the South Africans call their verandas. It was gin and tonic all round. She remarked, "I don't like to put the top back on the gin bottle. I think it inhospitable." That's a South African lady for you! The date was 7 October 1960, the day before the wedding. Nobody could understand how we had timed our arrival so precisely. We were rather surprised ourselves. We learned later that we were long spoken of in Johannesburg society as the two who had driven 20,000 miles for a glass of champagne.

Clive Turner, the bridegroom himself, was dumbfounded to have news of our arrival. He had long since dismissed our acceptance of his invitation as a joke, despite our sending him a postcard from India. When I telephoned him, he thought I was another Chris and gave me a list of things to do! He was speechless when he realised that we had arrived. Even today, I cannot appreciate how extraordinary had been our journey. Apologies that we had foregone going as far east as Calcutta and as far north in Africa as Ethiopia, seemed not to dull the sparkle of our tale. The parents of his splendid bride, Jill Matthews, held a drinks party that evening. Chris Augwin, a friend from university, was there too.

The wedding was a great success. It was held at St Martin's-in-the-Veld. Afterwards there was a fine party at the country club. On the morning of the wedding, the Augwins did tremendous work with finding John and me some clothes. John borrowed a suit from Clive and a dinner jacket for the country club from Chris Augwin's father. I was loaned both by the Osbornes whose son was away.

The referendum had given a four per cent (or 70,000) victory for the republicans to the disappointment of those with largely English connections. At the end of the reception, "God Save The Queen" was sung with more fervour than usual. Everybody was extremely politically conscious. An outsider's opinions were assumed to be anti-apartheid and the entertainers began arguing from there. Opinions were often more hysterical than profound and realistic. The truth was that the British people were in understandable anguish. They believed that should voting become universal, then the nation's prosperity would be damaged. If it did not, then there would be bloodshed.

John and I both left Johannesburg on the morning of 13 October 1960 – John for England by air and myself five hours later on a road trip to Durban and then via the Garden Route to the Western Cape to complete our expedition's total distance of over 16,500 miles in some seventeen weeks.

Only Nairobi had showed the development I now experienced in South Africa, as evidenced by the new fully tarred, well-surfaced road to Pietermaritzburg, the capital of Natal. I called in at Newcastle, a town before the capital, on the way and visited the local Austin agent, Mr Mackenzie. He corrected a problem with the rear wheels and was thrilled to see the name "Murray and Charlton, Newcastle, England" on the dashboard.

Friends, and those I met for the first time, were as hospitable in Durban as in Johannesburg. I stayed with Betty and James Burt. Betty was my mother's friend from when they were bachelor girls in London years before. James got me temporary membership of the country club. This was a good start then. The Norths, the Butchers, the Orrs, the Forresters, the Brabys and Pauline James, they and more gave me as wonderful a time as if I were their own. I found it hard to understand how impressed they were with the trip we had made when it seemed so normal to me – just 15,000 miles. I really missed out on those wonderful South African girls, though, whose friendships I was too shy to progress.

I planned to take the Garden Route to Cape Town which roughly skirts the coastline and is celebrated for its beauty. South of Durban lies Transkei, then Pondoland. In Transkei, there was a huge storm – the sky went black and was ripped by forked lightning, giving a real torn curtain effect. Then it cleared to reveal a beautiful landscape and handsome Pondolese people walking the roadside in their blanket-like cloaks.

I passed East London and went through to Grahamstown where there is a famous school and Rhodes University with 1,400 students at that time. Here, Robin Matthews, the brother of Jill Matthews who married Clive Turner in Johannesburg, looked after me with his student friends. They found me a bed space on the floor in their room for my sleeping bag and I slept well enough. On my own, I had elected to stay at hotels on this leg of the trip, unwilling to camp alone, thus it was a welcome budget relief, although the hotels were first class.

Port Elizabeth is a little more than halfway between Durban and Cape Town, a distance of around 1,050 miles. I called there at the Goodyear Tyre Centre to show off our tyres which had needed no renewal in 16,000 miles. They took photos and details and sent us across to Mr Murray in charge of the Austin agents. He took great interest. "Come on, Mr Fenwick," he replied in response to my normal reticence, "this doesn't happen every day, you know."

But I was gone by noon on the way to Cape Town. Miles away, stopping at Ootshorn for the night, I was in the hotel dining room alone, the other guests having finished and moved on (hotels finished dinner by seven o'clock in Africa). Here I had my only political conversation with a black African.

"Where are you from?" enquired the waiter.

"England."

"My goodness – you are free."

"Are you not?"

"No, we cannot move."

That was the only non-white social opinion I obtained in South Africa. It was significant.

I went to the phone and rang Douglas Duncan, my distant relative in Cape Town. I had not given him much notice of my impending arrival but he had been a guest of my parents in England.

Our conversation went something like:

"Hello, do you remember me? I am Christopher Fenwick."

"Yes I do. To what do I owe the pleasure?"

"I am in South Africa, may I come and see you?"

"Yes, of course, but my wife Beavie is in England. I am on my own. Are you able to stay? Where are you?"

"Ootshorn ..."

"What on earth are you doing there? How did you get there?"

"I drove."

"Where from?"

"From Cambridge, England."

There was a long silence then, "Good God, good God. Which way did you come?"

"By Iran and India, then crossing to Aden." I could never comprehend that this would surprise people.

"Good God, you must come and stay."

Douglas was not a social man, perhaps Cape Town

was not as social as Durban. He was bookish (he ran an excellent bookshop called Juta), withdrawn and thoughtful. He took a dark view of South Africa's future and could not see how bloodshed could be avoided in the future. The time for compromise had passed, he felt, when the elections of 1948 had put the Nationalists firmly in power. Happily this was avoided, but the decline in political and economic administration had been inevitable.

He turned to the drinks cabinet: "Have you tried the Cape drink, cognac and Canada?" Brandy and ginger, or a "horse's neck". We drank a few.

He accompanied me around Cape Town. He showed me his bookshop and the best books on South Africa. He told me how to put the car on the ship back to England. The process was trouble free. I left it with *RMS Edinburgh Castle* and picked it up two weeks later in Southampton.

For me, I had found a French Airline, UAT (Union Aéromaritime de Transport) to fly me to Paris. I can't remember what its advantage was – perhaps because it flew a DC-8 rather than a Boeing 707 from Johannesburg to Paris by way of Salisbury and Brazzaville. The sight of the Congo River as we climbed away from Brazzaville, where we touched down en route, must make it one of the most dramatic take-offs in Africa.

I flew to Johannesburg, stayed the night with Chris Augwin, my friend from Pembroke College who had also hosted us generously during our week there, and left the following morning. To my surprise, my parents, whom I had kept informed of my plans, had come to Paris to meet me. It was good of them. They took me to Harry's Bar and to dinner afterwards. Nearly twenty weeks of expedition had been undone in a day. But oh, how I missed out on those South African girls!

Epilogue

The earth has circled the sun nearly fifty-seven times since Robin, John and I motored east and south of Cambridge, England. We have told of the "political window" that brought us relative security in the countries that formed our route in 1960. Our timing was well chosen; the window did not last the decade.

It is remarkable to reflect today that Pakistan, India and Ceylon (Sri Lanka) had been under the British Crown a little more than a dozen years beforehand. In addition, our path from Aden to Cape Town was still under the British Crown. Such had been the extent of former British imperial rule that its former lands covered just under two thirds of our journey by road.

We did not drive, as we had hoped, as far east in India as Calcutta (Kolkata), nor reach as far north in Africa as Eritrea and Ethiopia before journeying to Cape Town. Instead, our easternmost point was Varanasi (Benares), India and our northernmost in Africa was Eldoret, Kenya. Nonetheless, the route we had painted on the bonnet and rear door of the car of "Cambridge – Colombo – Cape Town" was completed, and in time for Clive and Jill Turners' marriage in Johannesburg.

Some might say that we suffered bad luck with the motor car. The choice of car, however, had always been part of the challenge. As noted, plenty of people had driven to India in overland vehicles such as Land Rovers, and a number had made the trip with production saloons. Some had even driven the two continents in Land Rovers, but we could find nobody who had driven the two continents in a "small family saloon". This was the challenge. It proved a bigger one than we ever thought, but then fortune smiled upon us.

Fortune smiled upon us through the near universal curiosity, generosity and kindness of the people we came across. A good many of them, but not all, were garagistes towards whom we inevitably directed ourselves whenever we arrived in a town of any size, at least after the Turkish border where we met our first breakdown. Our expedition was greatly strengthened, heartened and enriched by such people.

Nick in Belgrade, Ali Tobraki in Tabriz, Mr Monti in Tehran, the man who fitted Jeep U bolts in Shiraz, Mr Talbot in Rawalpindi, the chief of police in Peshawar, Mr O'Brien in Delhi and, outstandingly, the works manager of the TVS Garage in Trichinopoly after my collision with the rock fifteen miles north of the town. He came out at three in the morning with his truck, loaded the car, returned it to his garage and, with his entire squad of mechanics, charged us £30 for working a three day bank holiday weekend to repair the damage. The same series of welcomes awaited us in Aden and Africa starting with Horace Gow in Nairobi.

I find it almost embarrassing to talk about the expedition expenses. There were complaints at the time about the mild inflation of the fifties, but this was at an annual level of only three per cent. It was not until the seventies that severe inflation took place, with prices quadrupling in eleven years.

As to our costs, the most costly item was the "small family saloon", the Austin A40, which we bought new for £641 and, on our return, sold it back to our dealers, Murray and Charlton, in Newcastle for £435 – a deficit of £206. The passage – Colombo to Aden for John, myself and the car on P&O's *SS Strathnaver* – was £221, while the only other expense we had of more than £50 was insurance which totalled £87. The price for bringing the car back to Southampton was £47.

These days, the Middle East, India and Africa are littered with intercontinental hotels charging room rates similar to those in the West End of London. They are very different from the "best places" that we encountered in towns where we stopped along the way. These were more homely and moderately priced. Prices in Britain were low, too, in comparison.

The night before we left, we entertained our parents to dinner in Kensington, nine of us for a total bill of £14.50. The next morning, we flew our car and ourselves by an airline called Silver City from Lydd in Kent to Calais for £13. We began by putting £500 each into a kitty, adding £150 when we reached Aden. We represented this by letters of credit, traveller's cheques and foreign currencies. Apart from flights home, the entire trip cost us less than £2,000, including the shipping and the car. Fuel was, incredibly, less than £100!

I have never returned down that oriental road, but both John and Robin have, although at different times.

After working at De Havilland, in 1967 John joined two friends to enter a Ford Escort two litre in the London–Sydney Marathon car rally, driving to Bombay, then taking ship to Fremantle, Western Australia, before driving to Sydney. Halfway across the Nullarbor Plain, they "hit a bump" which moved the engine rearwards from its mountings. John, well-practised by this time, put things together again and drove on to Sydney.

John went into manufacturing and then into retail, in trading at first and then property. He retired and took to yachting, buying a boat ("more like a Ford Granada rather than a Rolls Royce"). He loosed from Lymington one sunny October day, sailed south "and turned right when the butter melted". He sailed past Barbados and reached the Grenadines. Thence, he sent a list of fortnights to his friends inviting them to join him. Robin, myself and our wives were one of the first parties to go out; it was delightful.

Robin, passing his exams with flying colours, qualified as an architect and took a six month teaching position in Ahmedabad, South India, driving out there with Marianne whom he had just married. She went back early to prepare for a baby. He drove back "rather fast", bringing with him the son of the principal of the college who later went to Canada and set up a successful practice in Toronto. Inheriting agricultural assets, Robin became a farmer, first in Normandy and then in North Yorkshire.

My brothers and I had long since decided that we had a wonderful legacy in our family firm of department stores, and that we would let the side down if we did not make more of it. With some splendid colleagues, we expanded the stores and departments, welcomed the age of the consumer and surfed the waves of inflation. The expedition had taught us the excellent importance of completing a journey once planned.

We were thrilled to have the "small family saloon" complete the journey that we had planned for it. We had rightly judged that the window in our lives coincided with the political window that allowed us to drive safely by roads bordered by such wonderful peoples.

May peace be upon them or return to them indeed. They deserve it.

Appendix

Approximate Miles, Overnights and Costs

Asia total by Road	Miles
Cambridge to Istanbul	2,003
Istanbul to Tehran	1,743
Tehran to Nok Kundi	1,798
Nok Kundi to Srinagar via Afghanistan and Lahore	2,191
Srinagar to Delhi	555
Delhi via Jaipur, Agra, Cawnpore, Lucknow, Benares, river detours, Allahabad	799
Allahabad to Bombay	912
Bombay to Madras	826
Madras to Colombo	633
Asia total	11,460
Africa total by Road	Miles
Nairobi to Kampala and return	1,016
Nairobi to Copperbelt	1,650
Copperbelt to Johannesburg	1,521
Johannesburg via Durban to Cape Town	1,407
Africa total	5,594
Total by road	17,054

By Air and Sea	Miles
Lydd to Calais (Silver City Airways)	100
Colombo to Aden (*SS Strathnaver*)	2,200
Aden to Mukeiras and return (Aden Airways)	500
Aden to Nairobi (Royal Air Force)	1,200
By air and sea	4,000
Total all mileage	**21,054**

Overnight accommodation (20 weeks)	
Camping and rest houses	53
Hotels	37
Houseguests	36
On water (houseboat and *SS Strathnaver*)	11
Driving	4
Total	141

Total Costs	£
Kitty contribution @ £500 each	£1,500
Further contribution to kitty	£150
Cost of car at purchase £641 Sale on return £435 Net cost	£206
Fuel costs (included in above)	£100
Total Costs	**£1,856**